W9-BEE-230

Social Science in Government

SOCIAL SCIENCE

IN

GOVERNMENT

Uses and Misuses

RICHARD P. NATHAN

Basic Books, Inc., Publishers

NEW YORK

Library of Congress Cataloging-in-Publication Data

Nathan, Richard P.
  Social science in government.

  "April 7, 1988."
  Includes index.
  1. Social sciences—Research—United States.
2. Policy sciences—Research—United States.   3. United
States—Politics and government—1945–   . I. Title.
H62.5.U5N34   1988   300'.973   88–47668
ISBN   0–465–07911–3

Copyright © 1988 by Basic Books, Inc.
Printed in the United States of America
Designed by Vincent Torre
88 89 90 91 RRD 9 8 7 6 5 4 3 2 1

For Mary

CONTENTS

Contents

PREFACE

BEFORE YOU READ THIS BOOK, I will reveal the secret strategy that guided me in writing it, though once I do this, my cover is gone. This book is about applied social science research in the domestic governmental process in the United States. It looks at the history of applied social science since the mid-1960s. As a participant-observer, I put forward a positive point of view and a set of specific prescriptions for the future.

I would like to influence my fellow practitioners in the business of public policy research, but—here is my secret strategy—I attempt to do this *indirectly*. The book is written to appeal *directly* to three audiences. I hope to teach the first audience, students of social science and social policy, about the rudiments, experiences, and important lessons of efforts to apply social science wisdom to social policy in America. The ups and downs, successes and failures, and good and bad practices are described here using specific studies to bring my subject to life in what I hope is an exciting way.

The second group of readers I want to influence directly are the users of social science research. I think I know what you should demand, and if you agree, I believe your efforts can make social science a more valuable input to social policy. Government officials, legislators, staff experts, outside experts, and consultants—to all of these groups—I would like to suggest new ways of thinking about the uses and usefulness of applied social science research.

The third group I want to influence directly is the funders of applied social science research, including both government and foundation officials. You are in the catbird seat between social science and social policy. I want you to demand this product. I also want you to shift your demand curve in particular ways that will influence the supply. Throughout this book, I advance a set of proposals for changes in the organization and conduct of applied social science research. These recommendations involve the selection of the subjects to be studied, the scale and character of the studies conducted, the selection of the people to participate in them, the way such people are organized, and the research methods and types of data they use. In all of these respects, my aim is to press for changes that I believe, based on experience in the field, can enhance the usefulness of applied social science research and at the same time contribute to social science scholarship.

If I succeed in this enterprise, my fellow social science researchers will have to read this book, or at least they will have to know about it. What did Richard Nathan tell the people who fund social science research to do? Why are grant officers making these requests and asking us these questions? Should we adopt Nathan's ideas, and how could we do so? So there you have it. The secret is out; my strategy is revealed.

Yogi Berra once said, "You can observe a lot of things just by watching." His comment is relevant to this book in two ways. In the first place, the basic approach to social science research, both applied and theoretical, that I advocate here emphasizes immersion in the subject matter—*observation, watching.* My strong orientation is toward empirical research that makes extensive use of facts about people's lives. Social scientists should work in the laboratory of life, with a deep, genuine, and personal understanding of the subject being studied. Lest there be any mistake about it, I should state at the outset that I am concerned about the abstract, often exclusively theoretical, research and writing about subjects or phenomena that social scientists say are "policy relevant" even though they have never encountered them in the real world.

In the second place, Yogi Berra's comment applies to the organization and subject matter of this book. As mentioned earlier, I rely heavily on specific research projects that I have worked on or observed to derive lessons for the future practice of applied social science. One of my major sources is a series of evaluation studies I conducted with colleagues at the Brookings Institution in Washington, D.C., and at the Urban and Regional Research Center of the Woodrow Wilson School at Princeton University. These studies focus on the effects of national domestic policies and programs on state and local governments and the people they serve.

A second major source of research experience is the work of the Manpower Demonstration Research Corporation, founded in 1974 with the support of the Ford Foundation. This corporation, based in New York City, which currently has a staff of nearly one hundred people, conducts demonstration studies to test new programs that deal with the problems of society's most disadvantaged groups—groups many experts today would categorize as part of the "underclass." I have been a member of the board of directors of the Manpower Demonstration Research Corporation since its establishment. I admire the work done by its extraordinary staff, dedicated to applied research that makes a difference. At the same time, I want to make it clear that I have not directly participated in the conduct of these studies. My descriptions of the lessons to be drawn from these studies represent my own views and are not meant to represent the ideas or views of my fellow board members or the staff members of the Manpower Demonstration Research Corporation.

My greatest intellectual debt for this book is to these two

groups, my research colleagues at Brookings and Princeton and the board and staff of the Manpower Demonstration Research Corporation. I also want to express my appreciation to others in the field of social policy research, many of them friends of long standing, who willingly (and in some cases without realizing it) have influenced me and shaped my ideas. Scores of people, many of them mentioned along the way in this book, have produced the research on which this book is based. Specifically, I express thanks to colleagues past and present who have read parts of this manuscript and provided reactions and suggestions: Orley C. Ashenfelter, Rebecca M. Blank, Robert F. Cook, Martha A. Derthick, Paul R. Dommel, Eli Ginzberg, David A. Long, Gilbert Y. Steiner, Donald E. Stokes, Aaron Wildavsky, and Michael Wiseman.

The Ford Foundation and the Schumann Foundation provided financial support for this work, much of it conducted in a sabbatical year. Special appreciation is due Susan Berresford and Shepard Forman of the Ford Foundation and William Mullins of the Schumann Foundation. Martin Kessler at Basic Books was a patient critic and reservoir of helpful advice. Suzanne L. Wagner at Basic Books served ably as project editor for this book. Nan Nash, my secretary, helped me to put so many versions of the manuscript into our word processors that I think together we could recite it from memory. I thank her very much. Jonathan Jacobson and John Lago proofed the manuscript, and John Lago provided valuable research assistance as well. My wife, Mary, has provided useful counsel and much-needed support and encouragement. I thank her most of all.

—RICHARD P. NATHAN
Princeton University

Social Science in Government

I

The Role of
Social Science in Government

AMONG WESTERN NATIONS, the United States stands out for the optimistic, almost euphoric, belief on the part of social scientists and many politicians that social science scholarship can be useful in the governmental process. The commitment to this idea had its heyday from the mid-1960s to the mid-1970s. Social scientists were feeling their oats. Economists were prominent in government; they were instrumental in the development of national economic policy and in Lyndon Johnson's war on poverty. There was a feeling of ebullience about the potential for applied social science in national domestic policy.

That optimism has faded. In recent years political leaders have been less willing to apply social scientific knowledge in a systematic way in government. How did the social scientific revolution in government come into being? What were its main purposes and manifestations? Why has applied social science fallen from grace? Where do we go from here? The focus of this book is on the effort to make social science a handmaiden of the governmental process.

There is an abbreviation used in movie scripts—POV—that stands for "point of view," referring to the angle of the camera in a particular scene: Who is doing the looking and what do they see? In the field of public policy research, I think it would be a good idea to require all authors to begin by describing their "POV," stating right up front what their "camera angle" is.

I have spent two decades as both a producer and a consumer of public policy research in the field of U.S. domestic affairs. This includes substantial periods as a researcher, teacher, and government official. As a staff member of the Brookings Institution from 1972 to 1979, I directed a series of field evaluation studies of federal grant-in-aid programs—revenue sharing, block grants, the public service jobs program, among others. On the other side of this transaction between social science and social policy, I was an official of the U.S. Office of Management and Budget and the Department of Health, Education, and Welfare during the first term of the Nixon administration, which (although it is often forgotten) was an exciting period of innovation in domestic affairs. I continue to have an active interest in shaping domestic policies, especially in the fields of welfare and employment. Since 1974, I have been a member of the Board of Directors of the Manpower Demonstration Research Corporation, which has conducted pioneering public policy research in these two fields.

These experiences, along with the published accounts of other public policy research projects, are brought together in this book to determine the usefulness of applied social science research in government. My attitude toward applied social science is both positive and optimistic. We have made mistakes. Nevertheless, I believe we can learn from these mistakes and make public policy research more effective. This book concentrates on one type of applied social science as an input to the governmental process—*research*. This input is often the basis of the expertise that gives social scientists their credibility in providing advice in the domestic policy process.

In domestic public affairs in the United States today, there is a spirit of disillusionment about the idea of applied social science research. In 1979 two sociologists published a book with the title *Why Sociology Does Not Apply.* [1] Another book on which I draw heavily depicts public policy research as having a "corrosive" effect on the policy initiatives of the Great Society period.[2] In a similar vein, Charles Murray in his provocative critique of social policy, *Losing Ground,* says that evaluation reports on Great Society programs, to the extent they were read at all, "led to a rapid loss of innocence about what could be expected from the efforts to help people escape from welfare dependency."[3]

There is, however, some solace. Accounts of well-publicized failures of public policy research have begun to be replaced in the media by reports on public policy research projects that have made a difference, studies that have been believed and used by politicians.

My interest is in both the substance of public policy research and the political process involved in deciding what to study, providing the necessary resources, and disseminating the results. In this chapter, I present the themes that are basic to my point of view about how applied social science research can be useful and used in the policy process. The first point is a simple one: social scientists by the very nature of their subject matter must have a close-up, real-time understanding of what they study.

Near the end of *Gulliver's Travels,* Jonathan Swift has a wonderful piece of satire meant to apply to the British Royal Academy that makes this same point. He describes Gulliver's voyage to Laputa and his visit to its major metropolis of Lagado. Everything in the Kingdom of Laputa is in terrible condition. "I never knew a soil so unhappily cultivated, houses so ill contrived and so ruinous, or a people whose countenances and habit, expressed so much misery and want." A major feature of Laputa is that there "is not a town of any consequence in the kingdom" that does not have its own academy. "In these colleges, the professors contrive new rules and methods of agriculture and building, and new instruments and tools for all trades and manufacture," so that "all the fruits of the earth shall come to maturity, at whatever seasons we think fit to choose, and increase a hundred fold more than they do at present." The only inconvenience, says Gulliver, is that "none of these projects are yet brought to perfection; and, in the meantime, the whole country lies miserably waste." Gulliver is permitted to visit the Grand Academy of Lagado where the first person he meets is a man "with meagre aspect, with sooty hands; his hair and beard long, ragged and singed in several places." He explains that he has been "eight years upon a project for extracting sunbeams out of cucumbers, which are to be put into vials hermetically sealed, and let out to warm the air, in raw inclement summers." In eight more years, he tells Gulliver, he shall no doubt succeed. But in the meantime, he pleads with Gulliver to "give him something as an encouragement to ingenuity, especially since this had been a very dear season for cucumbers." Concludes Gulliver, "I made him a small present, for my lordship had furnished me with money on purpose; because he knew their practice of begging from all who go to see them."[4]

My reason for beginning with this story is to emphasize that social scientists should venture forth from their academies to undertake innumerable happy projects, which unlike cloistered efforts to extract sunbeams from cucumbers, will have more immediate uses. Unfortunately, the application of social science to real world problems, however desirable, is not as easy to implement as it is to indicate.

Types of Applied Social Science

Looking back at the record of the 1960s and 1970s, one is hard put to define systematically the types of efforts to apply social science in government. Several groups of social scientists with varied purposes and approaches have attempted to apply their particular brand of social scientific wisdom in the public sector. I find it useful to distinguish three roles that social scientists play in government: policy analysts, researchers, and advocates.

I list policy analysts first because their role is the key to the definition of the other roles. Policy analysis was the basis of the effort by Lyndon Johnson in the mid-1960s to replace the traditional budget process with a programming-planning-budgeting (PPB) system that highlighted rational decision making. Economists trained as policy analysts entered the federal service in large numbers to staff the PPB system. But policy analysis, as it turned out, could not provide definitive answers. The enthusiasm of the 1960s about the widespread application of policy analysis in government proved difficult to implement in practice, to say the least.

Whether we like it or not, in most situations in modern government policymakers act on the basis of their beliefs and judgment because they lack the kind of knowledge that would enable them to base decisions instead on scientific evidence. Rather than evolving into a system founded on the widespread application of policy analysis to examine an array of alternatives and pick the one proven to have the greatest efficacy to meet some particular objective, policy analysis in government has become more of an art than a science. This is what Karen Davis means when she says policy analysis "relies on informed judgment." Policy analysis, according to Davis, can never replace political judgment.[5]

Aaron Wildavsky, writing on the art and craft of policy analysis, goes further than Davis but is on the same track. To Wildavsky, policy analysis is an interdisciplinary form of persuasion that involves "presenting a preferred policy in the most appropriate manner, by finding arguments that will appeal to others." Wildavsky adds, "How to help ourselves gain access to public life without becoming politicians is the challenge."[6] Indeed, this an enormous challenge.

I can sharpen this point about the limits of applied social science by listing five types of information, singly or in some combination, on which politicians base decisions. Politicians can, as just indicated, make decisions according to their beliefs: "This is the right thing to do." Or, they can base decisions on public opinion: "This is what my constituents want me to do." Third, they can rely on the advice of experts who have deep knowledge of a particular subject or issue. Fourth, they can on a more systematic basis ask for and use policy analysis—that is, studies specifically undertaken to define and assess major policy alternatives. Fifth, they can go one step further and use the results of applied social science research as a basis for decision making. It is this fifth input to policymaking—applied social science research—that is the focus of this book.

How is applied social science *research* different from policy analysis? Some of the easy answers to this question are not satisfying. One could say, for example, that social science research involves creating new knowledge or theories on which government officials can act with some confidence. This definition of research grounded in the traditional idea of science suggests an activity that is nonjudgmental; it involves establishing proof and having a specified level of confidence in the predictive power of a given research finding or set of findings.

However, not all applied social science research fits this classical idea of science: we cannot draw a line between policy analysis and research on the basis that policy analysis is judgmental and research is nonjudgmental. We have little choice but to distinguish research from policy analysis on more pragmatic grounds. I use three factors to define social science research and to distinguish it from policy analysis—its size, what one might call its "style," and its auspices. Applied social science research is *bigger* and it *takes longer* than what policy analysts do. It is also more likely to be done *outside of government*. It emphasizes a systematic, independent search for answers. Unlike most of the work of policy analysts, it is not tied to a particular set of policy objectives.

I believe that most of the literature on social science research as an input to government policymaking is too abstract and diffuse. Much can be gained by looking closely at specific studies and the history of major types of public policy research in charting a future for applied social science in government. In presenting my ideas about the relationship between social science research and social policy, I cover a range of applied social science research, but I concentrate on studies in the areas I know best. My examples are primarily in the twin fields of employment and welfare policy. Welfare reform is an especially important area of U.S. domestic policy; it has been an object of debate for more than a quarter-century. From a disciplinary point of view, I am most interested in the social science practitioners who have been prominent in efforts to conduct public policy research to be used in the governmental process, particularly economists, but also political scientists, sociologists, and psychologists.

Applied Social Science—A Two-Way Street

A major argument of this book is that the relationship between social science and social policy should be a two-way street. *The conduct of applied social science research is not only a matter of what social science can do for the real world. It is also and very much a matter of what the real world can do for social science.* Over the years social scientists have developed bad habits. Not only do I believe that applied social science can be useful to society, I believe it can be useful to academic social science by helping us to break, or at least mitigate, some of our bad habits. Three bad habits are discussed in this section.

The first bad habit of modern social science is the tendency to emulate the natural sciences. This often leads to spurious precision and an attitude toward theory building inappropriate for the real world. Beatrice Webb, who worked with Charles Booth in England on the development of survey research methods, considered this problem in her autobiography, called *My Apprenticeship,* about her life as a "social investigator." Webb's family had a close friendship with Herbert Spencer, whose elaborate theorizing about the wonders of unfettered capitalism could not have been more antithetical to the career and political path followed by Beatrice Webb. In *My Apprenticeship,* Webb used her relationship with Spencer to present her ideas about the meaning of social science. Referring to Spencer's writing, she said, "There was a riddle in the application of the scientific method to human nature which continuously worried me, and which still leaves me doubtful. Can the objective method, pure and undefiled, be applied to human mentality; can you, for instance, observe sufficiently correctly to forecast consequences, mental characteristics which you do not yourself possess?"[7]

This is the nub of the debate about the meaning of social science. Can we predict human behavior using "the objective method, pure and undefiled"? My view on this question can be summed up as as follows:

> The data simply do not exist, nor can they ever be collected, which would tell us everything we want to know about every attitude, emotion, and form of behavior of every individual and relevant group (or sample of same) in such a way that we could use them

to construct models that would produce theories that approach the predictive power of theories in the natural sciences, even allowing for the fact that the stereotype that social scientists often have of the natural sciences is overdrawn.

The second bad habit of modern social science is *overspecialization*. Modern social science is a bubbling pot of disciplines and subspecialties that have compartmentalized human society. In *Capitalism, Socialism, and Democracy,* Joseph Schumpeter stated, "Our time revolts against the inexorable necessity of specialization and therefore cries out for synthesis, nowhere so loudly as in the social sciences in which the non-professional element counts so much."[8] In a similar vein, Abraham Kaplan, in his brilliant book on methodology in the social sciences, was caustic in commenting on the fragmented, competitive character of the social sciences: "The fragmentation of science into 'schools' is by no means unknown in as rigorous a discipline as mathematics; what is striking in behavioral science is how unsympathetic and even hostile to one another such schools are."[9] This second bad habit of overspecialization is reflected in the organization of social science, both teaching and professional practice. The existence of rigid boundaries between fields and subfields is rooted in a reward system that measures achievement by one's ability to do independent work. One computer terminal in one cubicle is the most common organizational mode of modern social science.

The third bad habit of modern social science is closely related to the first two. I refer to the tendency of social scientists to strongly prefer quantitative research designs and techniques and in turn to downgrade qualitative research methods and data. Again, Abraham Kaplan's analysis is on target. Kaplan criticized what he called "the law of instrument": "Give a small boy a hammer, and he will find that everything he encounters needs pounding."[10] The hammer of modern social science is the computer. The individual social scientist in his

or her cubicle equipped with a computer terminal can work
with large data sets to demonstrate mastery of the latest bells
and whistles of mathematical practice that have mesmerized
the social science industry (other industries, too) in the computer age.

These bad habits of applied social science are deeply ingrained and addictive. But this is no reason to accept them.
Quite the contrary, much can be gained by efforts to shake
them. Applied social science should be part of the treatment.
I believe we can use applied research to overcome some of the
bad habits of modern social science. Not for a minute do I
envision such a widespread movement in this direction that it
would detract from the pursuit of theoretical social science in
academe. There is, of course, no danger of this, but the caveat
needs to be entered. There have been acrimonious debates
about the motives and judgments of intellectuals in the social
sciences who are involved in sponsored research. Such arguments have been too removed from actual experience; I believe
that close attention to specific cases can enable us to learn from
past practice in a manner that will contribute both to social
policy and social science.

Analytical Framework, Major Themes, and Organization

The analytical framework used in this book highlights three
types of applied social science research: (1) *studies of conditions and trends;* (2) *demonstration research* to test possible
new programs and policy approaches; and (3) *evaluation research* to assess the effects of existing programs. Most of my
attention is devoted to types 2 and 3, demonstration and evaluation research, on the premise that public policy research

should concentrate more on studies of *how to do things* than on what should be done. From my perspective, this means that priority should be assigned to applied social science research to test new ideas and to assess ongoing programs. These two types of applied social science research should be favored over studies of conditions and trends. Three other key ideas are central to the point of view of this book:

1. Demonstration and evaluation studies are *different* in ways that have not been sufficiently appreciated or taken into account by the sponsors of public policy research and by researchers. I believe evaluation studies are the frontier of applied social science. Social scientists interested in applied research in domestic affairs have more work to do, and more untapped potential, under this heading than in any other area of public policy research.

2. In designing and conducting both demonstration and evaluation research, greater attention should be given to *the missing links* of applied social science research. Two types of missing links are highlighted in this book—those between disciplines within the social sciences and those between quantitative and qualitative research methods and data.

3. In selecting the subjects for major demonstration and evaluation studies, priority should be given to situations in which the following *three conditions* apply. First, that policymakers are genuinely interested in the questions being asked. Second, they are uncertain about the answers. And third, they are willing to wait for them.

These ideas reflect a concept of social science that is both positive and at the same time limiting. I have cast applied social science as a supporting player, on stage occasionally and contributing in situations in which its character fits special circumstances. There are many parts of the drama of social action in which other players—beliefs, public opinion, expertise—have center stage. We have moved a long way from the optimism of the early postwar period, and from the notion that social science could be the basis for social engineering on a grand scale. Implicit in the earlier view was a Brave New World expectation that social science would replace what many intellectuals view as an inordinately competitive governmental process dominated by self-interest with a new process for rational decision making based on compelling evidence. But as is true for many experiences that generate passion, we have overreacted to the cooling of ardor. Academic social science has retreated into theory building. Increasingly, the highest prestige is accorded to mechanistic, often sterile exercises to generalize in ways that are far removed from life experience.

I submit, however, that a close look at the history of applied social science in the postwar period and its potential for the future suggests grounds for renewed commitment. This is not to say that applied research should be the main work, or even an important activity, of all social scientists. My position is that *more* social scientists should be drawn into *more* applied pursuits.

Daniel Patrick Moynihan, whose extraordinary career bridges the worlds of social science and public policy, said in 1969 that "the role of social science lies not in the formation of social policy, but in the measurement of its results."[11] This is the role of demonstration and evaluation research, as emphasized in this book. Three chapters are on demonstration research; two of these chapters deal in general terms with the history and conduct of demonstration research, and one presents case studies of recent demonstration research projects. Four chapters deal with evaluation research. Evaluation research turns our attention from tests of potential new programs (often studies of relatively small pilot programs conducted under controlled conditions) to studies of much larger public programs that have already been adopted.

Although the focus of this book is on demonstration and evaluation research, it is also necessary to consider the third category of public policy research, studies of conditions and trends as divided here into three subtypes.

The first subtype is broad-gauged essays that look across a major function or area of social or economic activity and focus on policy implications and recommendations. This kind of diagnostic and prescriptive writing by social scientists has burgeoned in recent years and in my view has been overdone. The problem is that social scientists serving in this role often behave too much like politicians. My concern is that the allocation of resources to large-scale projects to diagnose and assess social and economic conditions is not *as good a use* of a social scientist's time and energy as are other uses.

The second subtype of research on conditions and trends is modeling and projection studies that draw on existing data to analyze conditions in a given subject area or field of public policy. I have reservations about these studies, but less strong reservations than in the case of diagnostic and prescriptive studies.

The third subtype of applied social science research on conditions and trends involves primary data collection. I view such studies as the most desirable form of applied social science research under this general heading. In the field of social policy, a good example of a valuable original data set is the Panel Study of Income Dynamics (PSID) conducted by the Institute of Survey Research at the University of Michigan. Begun in 1968, the PSID is a large longitudinal survey that includes approximately 6,000 households. This survey, which oversamples poor households, has been widely used to study the characteristics and dynamics of the poverty population. A study using these data by Mary Jo Bane and David T. Ellwood illustrates the influence that this type of policy research can have. Bane and Ellwood, both on the faculty of the John F. Kennedy

School of Government at Harvard, used the PSID to study "spells of dependency" as an approach to research on welfare dynamics. Researchers and experts in the field now agree that this is the best way to analyze welfare dependency. The main conclusions reached by Bane and Ellwood point to a dual role for the Aid for Families with Dependent Children (AFDC) program, the principal welfare program for able-bodied adults and their children:

> We find that of all those women who begin a spell of AFDC receipt, half will have ended their spell within two years. At the same time over half the people who are receiving AFDC at any point in time are in the midst of a spell that will last eight years or more, and these women account for over half of the expenditures of the AFDC program.[12]

I want to be clear about the point I am making, which is to urge the greater allocation of resources for applied social science research to how-to-do-it studies. This entails a shift in the allocation of resources away from studies of conditions and trends toward larger-scale demonstration and evaluation studies, particularly those based on a synthesis of social science disciplines and quantitative and qualitative methods and data.

Taken as a whole, one of the best ways to support this point is to discuss the way the findings of social science studies of conditions and trends are often used. The typical practice among the organizers of hearings and conferences on social and economic problems is to pick a range of experts representing different positions. Whether the subject is unemployment, poverty, pollution, or the problem of child abuse, it is likely to be considered in a forum that allows for the presentation of a range of expert opinions. The reason this is done is that one's prior assumptions in studies of conditions and trends often affect one's conclusions. Values and preconceptions are less likely to be a factor—or at least they are likely to be less of a factor—in policy research once government officials have defined a problem and are engaged in the process of developing and revising policies for dealing with it.

To sum up, I believe applied social science research should emphasize questions involving *how to do things* rather than what should be done and that research should concentrate on the conduct of *demonstration* and *evaluation* studies. I am concerned about *two missing links* of applied social science research: the links between disciplines and between quantitative and qualitative research methods.

Combining social science disciplines involves much more than bringing additional types of data to bear in public policy research. It involves adding variables to the research equation. When we leave out disciplines in applied social science research, we often leave out variables that in many instances are of great importance to policymakers. A deeper point is also involved here. The problem of disciplinary compartmentalization often produces social science research, both theoretical and applied, that is so rooted in a single intellectual paradigm that it distorts human experience. A major plea of this book is for large-scale applied social science research projects that integrate disciplinary paradigms on a *system's basis* that aids both social policy and social science.

The second of the two missing links of applied social science research, that between quantitative and qualitative research methods, is closely related to the first. In the postwar period, economists have been the dominant participants in public policy research. The other disciplines that now need to be brought more extensively into such studies—psychologists, sociologists, and political scientists—tend to rely more heavily than do economists on qualitative research methods and data. This distinction is not one between using or not using numbers. It involves a preference on the part of economists for rigorous statistical techniques to assign levels of probability to statements of causality, rather than on research approaches, which are often empirical and numerical, but which deal with qualitative variables and causal relationships in less rigorous ways.

Establishing a new synthesis in the conduct of applied social science research in a manner that deals with these two missing links requires more than good arguments. We need to consider the organization and politics as well as the substance and methods of applied social science research. The role of the government and foundation grant officers responsible for selecting the subjects and researchers for applied studies is a critical one. These officials occupy the important position between the producers and the consumers of policy research. The final chapter of this book examines the role of the sponsors of public policy research, particularly grant officers; how they behave; and how their behavior might be changed in ways that affect both the selection of subjects and the conduct of applied social science research in the governmental process.

I began collecting material for this book in 1982. Since then I have taught two graduate seminars on the usefulness of applied social science research. In one of these seminars, a student asked why applied social science research is so strongly focused on social programs and particularly on programs to aid the poor. The student remarked, "Liberal advocates of social programs have shot themselves in the foot by emphasizing studies that often show the limits and pitfalls of social programs and only rarely their successes." The image is haunting. Applied social science research in many instances has ended up undermining the case for social programs. This is one of the reasons for the current disillusionment with applied social science in government and the pulling back from such efforts. However, the strongest opposition to applied social science has come, not from liberals, but from conservatives. Deep down I think the conservatives are justified in their doubts about applied social science. If social science researchers were to do their job properly and improve the design and conduct of applied research, I believe we can increase the ability of government to deal with and resolve social problems. But we have to change the way we do business if we want to get the social scientific revolution in government back on track.

2

The Rise and Fall of
Applied Social Science

IN THE IMMEDIATE postwar period in the United States, there was a decided increase in the interest of social scientists in applied work in the public sector. Leading authorities in the field urged closer linkages between social science and social policy. In the introductory essay in a volume on what were called "the policy sciences," Harold Laswell wrote in 1951, "It is probable that the policy-science orientation in the United States will be directed towards providing the knowledge needed to improve the practice of democracy."[1] Laswell's co-editor for this volume, Daniel Lerner, envisioned a future in which social science would deal with "the new human problems raised by the endlessly changing lifeways of modern society."[2] There is, said Lerner, "an integral connection between social science and social democracy."[3] Education in the social sciences in the 1950s was infused with this idea of improving social and economic conditions, often with the expectation that the different disciplines would work together in defining problems and devising solutions. Robert S. Lynd, in a book entitled *Knowledge for What? The Place of Social Science in*

American Culture, called for merging the work of the social sciences by focusing on the concept of culture. By culture, Lynd referred to "all the things that a group of people inhabiting a common geographical area do, the ways they do things and the ways they think and feel about things, their material tools and their values and symbols." Lynd saw this concept as meeting "the need for an all inclusive frame of reference for all the social sciences."[4] But Lynd's dream of a coherent multidisciplinary role for the social sciences would not materialize. From the early 1960s to the 1970s, when the effort to apply social science in government was in its heyday, one discipline, economics, tended to play the strongest role. Robert H. Haveman, in his history of poverty research from 1965 to 1980, notes, "For better or worse, the fact is that most social science research which was stimulated by the War on Poverty was in economics." In a tongue-in-cheek footnote, quoting a sociologist who reviewed his manuscript, Haveman says the reviewer agreed that economists played the central role, adding that "the viewpoint of those who bought the coffee is less central."[5]

It is useful to divide the move to apply economics to public policy in postwar America into three parts. First was the idea that Keynes's general theory of macroeconomics could be applied on an ongoing basis to produce steady noninflationary economic growth. The other two major types of applications highlighted microeconomics. The most ambitious effort to apply microeconomics in government was the comprehensive "planning-programming-budgeting" system to reform the budget process. The second and more focused way in which the ideas of microeconomics were applied in government was in the "evaluation research movement." The evaluation research movement involved large-scale research projects sponsored and funded by government to demonstrate possible new program approaches and to evaluate existing, ongoing programs. Despite the fact that these three developments emanated from the same tradition, were linked in execution, and often involved the same people, they are different in their organization and timing. The three efforts to apply economic concepts and methods in government are described in the sections that follow.

Applied Macroeconomics

Under President Kennedy, economists were prominent participants in the national economic policy process. A feeling of confidence emerged that the economy could be managed in a way that would repeal the business cycle and produce stable noninflationary economic growth on a long-term basis. In an unprecedented action, Kennedy in 1963 recommended what at the time was a large reduction in federal personal and corporate income taxes. He explicitly applied Keynes's theory to policy-making by deploying unused resources to create jobs and stimulate economic growth. After Kennedy was assassinated, Lyndon Johnson carried through on this proposal. Early in 1964, the Congress enacted a $16 billion tax reduction. Walter W. Heller, then chairman of the Council of Economic Advisors, who was both the principal architect of the tax-cut plan and an artful phrasemaker, described this economic policy as the nation "declaring a fiscal dividend" to combat "fiscal drag" in a faltering economy. The following year, Heller delivered the Godkin Lectures at Harvard University on the subject of the new role of economics in government. The first sentence set the tone: "Economics has come of age in the 1960s." Heller added, "The age of the economist arrived on the New Frontier and is firmly entrenched in the Great Society." The Keynesian influence was clear. Said Heller, "What economists have wrought is not the creation of a 'new economics,' but the completion of the Keynesian revolution—thirty years after John Maynard Keynes fired the opening salvo."[6]

Unfortunately, the business cycle, as it turned out, was not repealed. Stagflation (recession and inflation occurring simultaneously) in the 1970s generated major controversies among and between economists and politicians. The consensus on the Keynesian approach fell away. There was a great din of voices about new approaches, including the controversial supply-side strategy adopted in the Reagan years, which according to legend was conceived on a cocktail napkin. In any event, the high hopes of consensus macroeconomics skillfully applied in government that Heller described with such enthusiasm at Harvard in 1965 sound hollow in retrospect.

The application of macroeconomics in the U.S. government for the most part is carried out by professional economists working inside the government. At the highest levels, economists apply their knowledge in governmental decision making, for example, as members of the Council of Economic Advisors and the Federal Reserve Board and officials in the Treasury and the Office of Management and Budget. Participants in this process usually serve as what Harvard political scientist Richard Neustadt calls "inners and outers," that is, men and women who identify with a particular party or program and serve in government for a limited period of time at the pleasure of the president. I do not mean to oversimplify. A cast of thousands of kibitzing economists with different types and degrees of credentials participate in the economic policy process. But most of these outside participants advise "on the side" rather than on a full-time basis.

The Planning-Programming-Budgeting System

A second major development of the 1960s in the application of economics at high levels to decision making in government involved much larger numbers of economists working inside the government. I refer to Lyndon Johnson's effort in the mid-1960s to remake the budget process in the image of neoclassical economics by establishing the PPB system across the board in the executive branch. The planning-programming-budgeting approach was initially applied in the defense department by Robert S. McNamara, who had formerly been president of the Ford Motor Company and who was appointed by Kennedy as secretary of defense. McNamara and his staff of "whiz kids" used the PPB system to compare alternative weapon systems. In this way, they hoped to increase the leverage of the secretary of defense in relation to the individual services. Before the Vietnam War escalated, the widely acclaimed McNamara system was riding high. Johnson decided that this approach should be applied not just in the defense sector but in the domestic arena as well.

Characteristically, Johnson embraced the PPB system with gusto. In an executive order issued 25 August 1965, he directed that all agencies apply this approach to the budget process of the executive branch. The governmentwide PPB system announced by Johnson in August 1965 set forth ambitious requirements to take effect immediately: all federal agencies were to prepare planning documents and "issue-analysis papers" to back up their recommendations to the U.S. Bureau of the Budget. (This was before the Bureau of the Budget was reorganized and renamed the Office of Management and Budget under Richard Nixon.)

According to the *Bulletin* issued by the Bureau of the Budget to set up this new system, the objective of PPB was "to improve the basis for major program decisions in the operating agencies and in the Executive Office of the President. Program objectives are to be identified and alternative methods to be subjected to systematic comparison." The system consisted of three main types of reports to be prepared by each agency: (1) *Program Memoranda,* comparing the cost and effectiveness of major alternative programs and describing the agency's strategy; (2) *Special Analytic Studies* on current and longer-run issues; and (3) *Program and Financial Plans,* multiyear summaries of agency programs in terms of their outputs, costs, and financing needs over a five-year period.[7]

The experience of PPB was, to say the least, disappointing. The paper just did not flow, or else it overflowed. Federal agencies used familiar bureaucratic stratagems to continue to operate the budget process in the way that they were used to doing it. In some cases, they simply did not submit the required planning memoranda and issue-analysis documents. Agency officials and the staff of the Bureau of the Budget operated in these cases as if nothing had changed. In other cases, agencies used the tactic of swamping the Budget Bureau with thick planning documents and elaborate issue papers that few, if any, high officials of the submitting agency had even seen. These documents were sometimes sent to the Budget Bureau in large cardboard boxes containing material that could not possibly be read, much less thoughtfully considered, by agency officials.

I remember one such situation from my own experience as an official of the U.S. Office of Management and Budget (OMB) in the early 1970s. I was chairing a review of the PPB submission on health programs from what was then the Department of Health, Education, and Welfare. The material was formidable. A huge binder, which contained the Program Memorandum and Special Analytic Studies, was submitted by the agency along with a number of background papers and exhibits. These materials were submitted to us several hours before we were to meet with agency officials. There was no time to read it. The review meeting with agency officials, at which they referred to the binder and exhibits, was a wide-ranging, unstructured, and unsatisfying discussion of a wish list of program and policy changes. After the meeting, several OMB officials who were present (the author included) went back and read the submission, although in the normal course of business, pressing events and deadlines often made it impossible to do more than scan these materials. What we found was both sad and humorous. Pages were photocopies, in what sometimes appeared to be random order, of documents that senior agency officials probably had never seen. Some pages were upside down. The documents were unedited and sometimes undecipherable. Even the photocopying was poor. My OMB colleagues said this was an unusual case, but not that different from others.

Just a little over three years after Johnson's bold announcement of a governmentwide PPB system, President Nixon quietly issued a presidential memorandum abolishing the system: "Agencies are no longer required to . . . ," it said, and then it summarized the steps of the PPB system. Allen Schick, in an article on this nonevent (or at least relatively unnoticed event) called "A Death in the Bureaucracy," pointed out, "No mention was made in the memo of the three initials which dazzled the world of budgeting" when the PPB system was announced.[8]

Evaluation Research Movement

The third major development in the age of the economist is referred to by most observers as the "evaluation research movement," although, as already indicated, I believe a distinction should be made between the two main types of studies associated with this movement. Even though the evaluation research movement is closely allied to the PPB system, we need to separate these two developments. One reason has to do with the timing of this third major application of economics in government.

We tend to think of the age of the economist in government as coterminous with the Democratic presidencies of the 1960s and as having fallen off when the Republicans under Nixon came into office. It is true that PPB died a quiet death in the bureaucracy early in Nixon's presidency, but the other two developments discussed here, the application of macroeconomics and the evaluation movement, lasted much longer. It was Nixon who is supposed to have said, "We are all Keynesians now." Keynesian ideas strongly influenced the economic policies of his administration.

The timing of the evaluation movement, as it turned out, was decidely different from that of both applied macroeconomics and the PPB system. Because of the long period of time required to design, conduct, and report on large-scale demonstration and evaluation studies, the bulk of the work done under this heading was actually done in the 1970s, not the 1960s. Some of the major demonstration and evaluation studies, notably the negative income tax experiments featured in the next chapter, were begun in the late 1960s, but the results of these studies (planned and designed under Johnson) did not emerge until well after his presidency; most of the work was carried out in the Nixon period. Furthermore, a number of the biggest and most ambitious demonstration and evaluation studies were launched in the 1970s. The seeds of the evaluation movement were planted in the 1960s but were cultivated and bore their fruit a decade later.

Some commentators on the Nixon period have cited the interest in experimentation as a subtle, perhaps even cynical, strategy to use tests of new programs as a rationale for delaying their development or never enacting them into law. Yet a look at the record of new program adoptions, policy changes, and domestic spending in the Nixon years casts doubt on this interpretation. Large new programs were adopted under Nixon, and existing programs were expanded. Nixon may not have wanted us to say so, but he was a big spender on the home front. Total domestic spending of the federal government under Nixon rose from 10.3 percent of the gross national product at the outset of his presidency to 13.7 percent in 1974. Social Security accounted for 1.4 percentage points of this increase. Federal aid to state and local governments, which includes the revenue sharing and block grant programs that Nixon championed, also increased. Spending for federal aid to state and local governments accounted for a significant share (.8 percent) of the increase in the proportion of the gross national product devoted to domestic spending.

A second reason for treating the evaluation movement separately in this volume has to do with its organization. Unlike macroeconomic policymaking and the PPB system, the evaluation research movement for the most part involves people working *outside of government* in universities, independent research centers, and consulting firms. An army of external evaluators with economists in the vanguard marched to the tune of PPB. These battalions have conducted the major demonstration and evaluation studies.

Although PPB has departed from the scene, it left an important legacy in the form of the evaluation research movement. That legacy within government consists of what remains after the Reagan purges of the planning and evaluation staffs in federal agencies that were created to participate in the PPB process. These staff groups often were (and in many cases still are) the sponsors of demonstration and evaluation studies. Outside of government, the legacy of the PPB system is the army of public policy researchers who see their role as testing new social programs and evaluating old ones. Although in the Reagan period this army of researchers could be likened to George Washington's troops wintering at Valley Forge, a substantial corps of people in universities, think tanks, and consulting firms continue to work on applied social science in government.

One other point should be added to the ledger on the plus side as part of the legacy of the PPB system. It had a notable impact in making the budget process more analytical. It brought new people trained in economic analysis into the budget process. Many of them stayed on, and their contribution has been an important one. Nevertheless, the doubts that arose about the efficacy of macroeconomics as a policy guide and the failure of the PPB system to take hold on an across-the-board basis to bring microeconomics to federal budgeting were part and parcel of the dashing of the high hopes for applied social science in the years immediately following World War II.

It is not possible to pick an event or date that marks a turning point between the rise and fall of applied social science in postwar America. In the 1970s the critical commentary on the 1960s efforts to apply social science in government gradually gained momentum. Most remarkable was the breadth of this backlash. Concerns have been expressed by both liberals and conservatives, and they appear not only in the popular media, but also in academic writing. The remainder of this chapter considers these reactions. It begins with the most general commentaries, considers next the reasons for the demise of the PPB system, and then reviews in more detail the critical literature on the evaluation research movement.

New Criticism in Economics

Writing in the late 1970s, Carlos Fuentes, the Mexican Nobel laureate in Literature, said, "The science of economics is personal opinion converted into dogma, the only opinion that makes use of numbers to justify itself."[9] This attitude is manifested in complaints that economic models are out of touch with reality and reflect hidden biases about what is best and right for the society and the economy. My interest in this chapter, however, is not in popular expressions of skepticism about the application of economics in government, but rather in the questions raised by professional economists themselves. This literature, which I refer to as the "new criticism in economics," is directed at both first premises and methodology. It encompasses both macro- and microeconomics. Increasingly sharp questions have been directed at the "rational man" assumption in economic theory and analysis. As for methodology, the literature of the new criticism in economics is extensive. It is aimed at what many writers consider an overly rigid reliance on hypothesis testing and the strong preference of economists for mathematical modeling, in many instances grounded in statistical data that are not sufficiently precise to measure the conditions or behavior being studied.

The underlying question, as stated in the previous chapter, involves the degree to which the study of human behavior in the social sciences can be likened to the study of physical behavior in the natural sciences. This point is a central theme of a book on the limits of economics by Massachusetts Institute of Technology economist Lester C. Thurow. Economists, says Thurow, "can't find hard empirical constants, such as the speed of light in physics, because economists are not studying the immutable rules of nature but the mutable laws that govern human behavior."[10] Building on this observation, Thurow notes that mainstream economics reflects "more an academic need for an internal theoretical consistency and rigor than it reflects observable, measurable realities in the world we live in."[11]

The most famous statements associated with this literature of the new criticism in economics are by Nobel laureate Wassily Leontief, the inventor of input-output analysis and a former president of the American Economic Association. In his 1971 address as president of the American Economic Association, Leontief criticized his colleagues for their overemphasis on deductive theorizing and their failure to establish "systematic cooperative relationships across the traditional frontiers now separating economics from these adjoining fields." Leontief summarized his critique:

> In no other field of empirical inquiry has so massive and sophisticated a statistical machinery been used with such indifferent results. Nevertheless, theorists continue to turn out model after model and mathematical statisticians to devise complicated procedures one after another. Most of these are relegated to the stockpile without any practical application or after only a perfunctory demonstration exercise. . . .
>
> Continued preoccupation with imaginary, hypothetical, rather than with observable reality has gradually led to a distortion of the informal valuation scale used in our academic community to assess and to rank the scientific performance of its members.[12]

More than a decade later, Leontief repeated his criticism in even stronger terms in a letter to the editor of *Science* magazine. "The king is dead" but "no one taking part in the elaborate and solemn procession of U.S. academic economists seem to know it, and those who do don't dare to speak up." Leontief's concern in 1982 was twofold—the excessive use by economists of deductive and mathematical approaches, and, when they do empirical work, the use by economists of statistics to test economic theories where the statistics involved are inadequate to the task. "Page after page of professional economic journals are filled with mathematical formulas leading the reader from sets of more or less plausible but entirely arbitrary assumptions to precisely stated but irrelevant theoretical conclusions."[13]

Leontief's lament about the use of government statistics is especially pertinent for this book's stress on the need to combine quantitative and qualitative approaches in applied social science research. Leontief took his colleagues to task for their overreliance on government statistics "compiled for administrative or business, but not scientific purposes." These data, he said, "fall short of what would have been required for concrete, more detailed understanding of the structure and function of a modern economic system."[14]

A 1983 book by economist Andrew M. Karmarck echoes this same idea. Karmarck's concern is that economists "insist on quantification but completely overlook the need to understand how much precision is actually attainable in the accuracy of the numbers used. . . . Very little attention is paid to the quality of data—data are dumped into a computer without close examination." Sounding the same theme as Thurow, Karmarck points out that "forecasting future parameters or variables is incomparably more difficult in economics than in the physical sciences. . . . In fields concerned with human behavior like economics, in contrast, constant or stable phenomena can rarely be relied on."[15]

A comment on Leontief's 1982 letter, which created a tempest in the profession, was entitled "The Failures of Chair-Bound Science." In this article, economist Barbara R. Bergmann urged economists to broaden their scope of inquiry and in the process to rethink their position toward other and "softer" social science disciplines. "Economists might look with profit to the practice of social scientists in other disciplines, whose lower status and whose methods of research economists have been wont to scorn."[16]

Picking up on these themes, which are now widespread in the literature of the new criticism in economics, economist Robert Kuttner, in an article called "The Poverty of Economics" in *The Atlantic Monthly*, criticized economists for being "highly abstract, mathematical, and deductive *rather than curious about institutions."* Kuttner quotes Charles L. Schultze, like Leontief a former president of the American Economic Association, as saying, "When you dig deep down, economists are scared to death of being sociologists. The one great thing we have going for us is the premise that individuals act rationally in trying to satisfy their preferences. This is an incredibly powerful tool because you can model it."[17]

Although it reached its peak in a much earlier period, there was once a strong institutional school of economics in the United States that reflected Bergmann's and Schultze's comments about economists acting like sociologists. This institutional approach was grounded in the idea that institutions— collectivities of people—behave differently than the sum of the individuals within them. John R. Commons, whose work at the University of Wisconsin in the 1920s made him a leader in this field, emphasized the difference in the behavior of groups compared to individuals, and he criticized economic theories built exclusively on individual behavior and the assumption of the rational man.

Beyond Commons's approach, which tied economics to society and politics, a related and more recent approach ties economics to psychology. This approach, as set forth by Robert E. Lucas, Jr., of the University of Chicago, questions the ability of economists to forecast the future because they do not give adequate attention to attitudes and attitudinal shifts that influence behavior.[18] The Lucas critique was made a centerpiece of the "supply-side" challenge to contemporary macroeconomic theory by the Reagan administration in 1981. Keynes made this same point; he emphasized the psychological dimension in assessing the performance of economic systems. In the same vein, Albert Hirschman maintains that economists neglect mood and attitudinal variables. Hirschman believes that modern economics tends to oversimplify. He argues "against parsimony" in the discipline, claiming that the conventional approach to economics presents "too simple minded an account of even such fundamental economic processes as consumption and production."[19] These concerns are being debated in the classroom as well as in the literature. I asked a recent graduate in economics if graduate students at his university ever talked about this new criticism. He answered, "Do we ever talk about these issues? My God, that's all we talk about."

Donald McCloskey, an economist who has become a historian of his discipline, suggests that although these and other challenges to economics are far-reaching they are not insurmountable. In the lead article in the June 1983 *Journal of Economic Literature* McCloskey described the official methodology of economics as "modernism." Modernism for McCloskey refers to "the credo of Scientific Methods, known mockingly among its critics as the Received View," which "is an amalgam of logical positivism, behavioralism, operationalism, and the hypothetico-deductive model of science."[20]

But then McCloskey adds a twist to the argument. He says that in truth economists do not follow their official rhetoric, and it is a good thing they do not. "If they did they would stand silent on human capital, the law of demand, random walks down Wall Street, the elasticity of demand for gasoline, and most other matters about which they commonly speak." Looking at the role economists play in government, in business, and in their classrooms, McCloskey suggests that they have already crossed the great divide. "Economists in fact argue on far wider grounds, and should. Their genuine workaday rhetoric, the way they argue inside their heads or their seminar rooms, diverges from the official rhetoric."[21] McCloskey's point is that the behavior of economists is not so much the problem as what they pretend their behavior is.

Although I find McCloskey's argument reassuring, I think he overstates his case. It is true that when economists talk informally about the economy and public policy, they often take social values and political behavior into account. But this willingness to take other kinds of factors into account—"soft" real-world variables—does not carry over easily into the professional practice of economics. In fact, one is struck by a paradox: the sharper the criticism of economics as a discipline, the stronger the tendency for economics as a profession to retreat to arid theory building.

The Demise of the PPB System

Charles Schultze, mentioned earlier as suggesting that economists might usefully act more like sociologists, is an important figure in the story of the demise of the planning-programming-budgeting system. Schultze was at the forefront of the efforts in the 1960s to apply economics in government; he was director of the Bureau of the Budget when the PPB system was put in place. After leaving the Johnson administration, in a series of Gaither Lectures delivered at the University of California in 1968, Schultze described his experience implementing PPB.[22] These lectures are a fascinating retrospective on the application of microeconomics to government budgeting.

Schultze began his lectures by describing the aims and main elements of the PPB system. But it is what he did next that is most interesting. He addressed the critique of PPB associated with the views of Yale political scientist Charles Lindblom. Throughout his career, Lindblom has concentrated on the basically incremental nature of the American political process and the ways in which it is antithetical to rational analysis and the planning values embodied in the PPB system.

After setting forth the Lindblom critique of PPB, Schultze proceeded to grapple with Lindblom's incrementalist position. Some readers may find, as I did, that Lindblom seemed to come out the winner. Schultze indicated considerable sympathy with Lindblom's argument about the difficulty of specifying the objectives of a given program. This is a necessary precondition in assessing programs and comparing them according to the degree to which they achieve their objectives. Lindblom contended that in a great many cases the goals of public programs cannot be defined precisely because politicians are purposefully vague about their legislative objectives in the belief, often correct, that this will enhance their chances of achieving them.

Digging deeper into Lindblom's ideas about "the science of muddling through," Schultze said that the PPB approach must adapt to, and become part of, the political process. He added that this is what actually happened under Johnson. According to Schultze, "program planning and evaluation staffs in the agency head's immediate office, created by the PPB system, strengthen the role of the agency head in relations with the operating units." And then Schultze observed, "Cynics to the contrary notwithstanding, knowledge is power."[23] In effect, PPB made economists actors in the political process. This may have been a good thing, but it is different from the ideas of early advocates of applied social science to the effect that social science should stay out of the political thicket. Its inability to do so in the case of PPB may indeed have been a major reason for the demise of this budgeting and policy analysis system.

Other political scientists besides Lindblom, in writing about the PPB experience, consider first premises. Bertram Gross, for example, notes that a major problem was that "micro-economists who have repeatedly used the term effectiveness have been chary about admitting, let alone explicitly stating, that they have been engaging in attempts at cause-effect analysis." Gross continues: "Once this is brought into the open, it becomes clear that estimates of presumed results must take into account many possible causative factors other than the program under analysis, and that many such factors, being social, psychological, and political in nature, are not readily understandable in terms of economics, or any other single discipline."[24]

Another important aspect of the PPB system covered in Schultze's Gaither Lectures is the scope of the PPB system. Looking back, Schultze saw wisdom in narrowing the scope of PPB:

> I propose as a working hypothesis that analysis can operate with fewer constraints and can profit from a consideration of a wider range of alternatives in programs that produce pure public goods and do not directly affect the structure of institutional and political power than in programs that produce quasi-public goods, fundamentally affect income distribution, or impinge on the power structure.[25]

This is a substantial concession. It is hard to think of government programs, particularly domestic programs, that do not in Schultze's terms "fundamentally affect income distribution" and "impinge upon the power structure." One is reminded of the development of cost-benefit analysis in an earlier era by Harvard economist Otto Eckstein in studies of alternative water-resource projects. These studies were narrowly focused on specific projects. Commenting on the history of cost-benefit analysis, Roland McKean said that cost-benefit analysis is generally best for lower-level decisions involving "comparatively narrow problems of choice" where "the alternatives are usually rather close substitutes."[26]

To sum up this part of the story, the objectives of PPB of assessing and comparing the costs and benefits of alternative public programs on a systematic basis are desirable, but are far beyond what can be achieved in a comprehensive and thoroughgoing manner. In these terms the narrower evaluation research movement treated in the next section can be seen as a reaction to PPB. It is, in effect, a more modest effort to do part of what the PPB system was supposed to do. The evaluation research movement identifies those programs that warrant full-scale studies. Whether the choice of the topics for these special and intensive studies is based on the criteria proposed by Schultze or on some other criteria, the fact is that the PPB system could never have operated as ambitiously and comprehensively as President Johnson initially announced. The essential problem was one of overkill.

The evaluation research movement, including the interest that emerged in the late 1960s in doing systematic demonstration studies with random assignment, came *after* PPB and can be viewed as an offshoot of the PPB system. What it said was that *some* subjects should be selected for serious large-scale studies. Furthermore, this was to be done without adhering to the implicit objective (at least on paper) of the PPB system of evaluating and comparing all major uses of governmental resources.

Economist Richard R. Nelson has commented specifically on the relationship between the evaluation research movement and the PPB system. Sounding very much like Schultze and Lindblom, Nelson said, "It does seem fair to question . . . whether the new philosophy of experimentalism represents greater sophistication regarding the implications of models of optimization over time under conditions of uncertainty, or disguised acceptance of a strategy of muddling through."[27]

But even if we regard the evaluation movement as a fallback—that is, a more modest approach to the application of microeconomics in the governmental process—our problems are by no means solved. This will be obvious as we turn to the literature on the evaluation research movement.

Evaluating the Evaluation Movement

Throughout this survey on the backlash against applied economics in government, I have relied on the writings of respected, card-carrying members of the economics profession, who in many cases were themselves participants in the events described. As we consider the literature on the evaluation research movement, I follow the same practice, beginning with an extraordinary book, *Politics and the Professors: The Great Society in Perspective*, by Henry J. Aaron, a senior fellow at the Brookings Institution. Aaron was a high-level official on the planning and evaluation staff of the U.S. Department of Health, Education, and Welfare in the 1960s and served as the assistant secretary of the successor department for these functions in the Jimmy Carter years. His book concentrates on the two main types of applied social science research that are the focus of my analysis, demonstration and evaluation research.

The thesis and tone of Aaron's critique are notably pessimistic. His conclusion is that demonstration and evaluation research in the field of social policy is not only very difficult to do, but that these studies have often produced findings about program results that fall far short of what was promised by politicians. Aaron portrays evaluation as "a newly developed art" that "certified the ineffectuality of these programs," referring to the social programs launched in the Great Society period. Further into the discussion, Aaron adds, "Far from being an instrument for evenhanded, objective deliberation, evaluation was transmuted into 'forensic social science.' "[28]

An important political problem is highlighted in Aaron's analysis: even those social science evaluation studies that were carefully and effectively carried out (social science at its best) often revealed limited, if any, results. Assuming that most researchers believed not only in the utility of applied social science, but also in the value of the social programs being tested or evaluated, this is a gloomy situation from their vantage point.

Aaron sums up his views in the following terms: "The role that research and experimentation played in the demise of the simple faiths of the early 1960s was not accidental. The process by which R&E [research and experimentation] is created corrodes the kind of simple faiths on which political movements are built; this effect is particularly strong when, as in the 1960s and early 1970s, the actions of political leaders tend to destroy those faiths and events make them implausible."[29] Two words in Aaron's conclusion stand out. One is his accent on "faith" as the basis for the actions by politicians in the field of social policy; the other is his reference to research and experimentation as "corrosive" of the kinds of simple faiths on which political movements are built.

Several years after Aaron's book was published, he made a similar tongue-in-cheek comment about the role of evaluation research directed at the efforts of then-budget director David A. Stockman to cut spending on social research:

Mr. Stockman is making a grave mistake in trying to put us all out of work. He has not realized that we are *the instrumentality for inaction.* By diverting us to teaching rather than research or even to still more reputable ways of earning a living, he will make easier the growth of ideas for activist social change undisturbed by critical analyses when the mood of the country shifts.[30]

Aaron is by no means alone in expressing doubts about the politics, practices, and results of evaluation research. For example, Sar A. Levitan and Gregory Wurzburg, close students of this period, said of evaluation research:

> It is not just a question of obtaining better data or spending a few million more dollars on evaluations. The problem lies in the basic assumptions of the methodologies employed by most evaluations, and in the choice of who is entrusted with the task. This entire field remains an art. The much touted objective scientific conclusions of evaluations are too often found to be based on hidden political and social value judgments or personal interest.[31]

Richard F. Elmore reviewed the studies of youth employment and training programs and concluded: "The fact that we find it easy to discredit interventions that merely deliver services, but difficult to find scientifically valid solutions to chronic social problems, may mean that we have gotten too sophisticated in using the rhetoric of social science to justify social interventions."[32]

On the conservative side, Charles Murray, in his influential book *Losing Ground,* makes many of the same points as Aaron, Levitan, Wurzburg, and Elmore. He, too, served as an evaluator of social programs in the 1970s. Murray's book is best known for his conclusion (presented as a "thought experiment") that goes one step—a very big step—further than Aaron. He not only maintains that social programs enacted in the 1960s failed but that in some cases they contributed to the problems they were supposed to solve. Hence, Murray argues that many of these programs should be abolished. Murray contends that "white condescension towards blacks" took a form that undermines incentives to work, family structure, and self-esteem. His solution is "to repeal every bit of legislation and reverse every court decision that in any way requires, recommends, or awards differential treatment according to race, and thereby put us back on the track that we left in 1965." Murray is specific in naming the programs that should be eliminated as part of his program:

> The proposed program, our final and most ambitious thought experiment, consists of scrapping the entire federal welfare and income support structure for working-aged persons, including AFDC, Medicaid, Food Stamps, Unemployment Insurance, Worker's Compensation, subsidized housing, disability insurance, and the rest. It would leave the working-aged person with no recourse whatsoever except the job market, family members, friends, and public or private locally funded services. It is the Alexandrian solution: cut the knot, for there is no way to untie it.[33]

In developing his thesis, Murray devotes considerable attention to the evaluation research literature. One section of his book on the role of research is called "Hard Noses and Soft Data." In it, Murray says: "In the spirit of cost-effectiveness that McNamara has taken to the Pentagon, the early poverty warriors were prepared to be judged on the hardest of hard-nosed measures of success."[34] Murray adds, "Social scientists who had been at the periphery of the policy process—sociologists, psychologists, political scientists—had the answer: scientific evaluation. The merits of doing good would no longer rest on *faith*."[35] The reference here to faith parallels Aaron's conclusion. Murray concludes his critique of evaluation research this way: "Starting with the first evaluation reports in the mid-sixties and continuing to the present day, the results of these programs have been disappointing to their advocates and evidence of failure to their critics."[36]

If I had scrambled the foregoing quotations about the problems of evaluation research, the reader would be hard put to sort them out on the basis of which statements had been made by liberals and which by conservatives. One is reminded of the riddle once posed by Aaron Wildavsky: what is the difference, he asks, between the New Deal and the Great Society? The answer is *evaluation research.*

Yet, of all the critical commentaries on the evaluation research movement, the most despairing is from a paper by Gary Burtless and Robert H. Havemen called "Policy Lessons from Three Labor Market Experiments." The three experiments are the negative income tax experiments conducted in Seattle and Denver, the supported work demonstration undertaken by the Manpower Demonstration Research Corporation, and the Employment Opportunities Pilot Project carried out in the Carter years. Burtless and Haveman draw the following conclusion: "Our experience in the last fifteen years has taught us that large-scale experiments can be relied on to teach us something of value about the policy in question, but what we are taught can seldom be relied on to aid the cause of reforming or improving policy."[37] This is not all. They go on to say: *"There is a moral here, and it is illustrated by the three experiments we have considered: if you advocate a particular policy reform or innovation, do not press to have it tested."*[38] The picture that this suggests (Woody Allen should direct it) would have social scientists sitting around a table trying to decide which programs they dislike most in order to test them and thereby undermine their chances of adoption—if you will, "corroding the simple faiths" on which they are based.

Later on, I discuss one of the demonstration research projects considered in the article by Burtless and Havemen, the supported-work demonstration, as an example of good practice that moves in the right direction. This case demonstrates a significant point about the literature on evaluation research. *I think we have overreacted.* There are valuable lessons from this experience, which should be drawn upon to move ahead—not to turn away—from the application of social science in government.

3

Demonstration Research

WHEN THE MEMBERS of the House and Senate conference committee worked out the compromise on the 1983 emergency jobs bill (a bill to combat the 1981–82 recession), they added a provision at the behest of Jamie Whitten, chairman of the House Appropriations Committee, to include $33 million for a highway project *"demonstrating* how a two-lane road can be widened to four lanes." A reporter for the *New York Times* covering the conference committee noted, "Mr. Whitten refused to say so, but all of the conferees expect that the money will wind up in Mr. Whitten's home district."[1] No mention was made in the *Times* story of a research design or a comparison road to be used as a basis for determining the efficacy of this road-widening demonstration.

The use of the word "demonstration" in this way is not unusual. In some cases the guise of a research project is more elaborate, but the underlying aim is the same—to use the rationale of a demonstration research project to obtain funds for a project even though there is no or very little intention of studying the results systematically to decide whether a particular tested program should be replicated on a broader basis. This is emphatically not the meaning of "demonstration" used in this book. I am interested in demonstrations as a type of applied social science research systematically conducted under conditions in which independent, trained researchers apply their expertise to provide knowledge that can be used by policymakers in deciding whether to adopt a particular course of action or type of program. The line between such undertakings and demonstrations with an ostensible, but not genuine, research purpose is often more subtle than in the case of Whitten's highway project.

To clarify the meaning of demonstration research, the following section discusses the language used to define the treatments tested in demonstration studies: the way we think about their impacts, the counterfactual state, control groups, quasi experiments, comparison sites, simulation techniques, dependent and independent variables, and the replication or generalization of the results of demonstration studies. Some readers may already know these terms, but for those who want to understand what social scientists do under the heading of demonstration research, this vocabulary lesson is likely to be helpful.

The first and most significant demonstration research projects, which were central to the rise of applied social science in the postwar years in the United States, were the negative income tax experiments. This chapter pays special attention to the conduct and history of these demonstrations and their influence on American social policy.

The Language of Demonstration Research

A potential new program being tested in a demonstration research project is referred to as a *treatment.* The idea that we should find out what works is hard to quarrel with. In many situations, society will be better off if we test potential new programs before we commit resources to adopt them on a broad basis.

Researchers in a demonstration study seek to determine the *impact* of a potential new treatment by measuring selected characteristics of the members of the treatment group before, during, and after they have participated in a demonstration. These characteristics are then compared to the characteristics for a nontreated group of similar persons. Did the tested treatment make a difference? If so, what kind of difference and how much of a difference did it make?

The task of identifying an untreated group to be compared with the treatment group is known as establishing the *counterfactual state*. The counterfactual state indicates what would have happened had there been no tested treatment. It is impossible to know the counterfactual state for certain—that is, to have the same participants both participate and not participate in a tested treatment. Researchers attempt to get at this elusive phenomenon of the counterfactual state in several ways. One method is to have eligible participants assigned randomly—as in a lottery—either to a treatment group or to an untreated group. We refer to the untreated group as a *control group*.

The use of random selection in demonstration research originated in the 1950s. The techniques were pioneered by British statistician R. A. Fisher. This experimental approach, using a randomly selected control group to establish the counterfactual state, was used extensively in the field of medicine before it became widespread in the field of social policy. Now random assignment is strongly preferred over other research approaches among social policy researchers because it employs statistical techniques to establish causality and to assign a level of probability to the impact of a tested treatment. My view is that random assignment is a good approach. Indeed it is *the best* approach to demonstration research in the field of public policy; nevertheless, U.S. social scientists have tended to go overboard in advocating it. In other Western countries, the idea of conducting social experiments with random assignment has not taken hold as it has in the United States.

Random assignment is not always used in demonstration research in the field of public policy in the United States. Researchers also use what are called *quasi-experimental* methods. Thomas D. Cook and Donald T. Campbell define quasi-experimental studies in precisely these terms—that is, as demonstration studies that do not use random assignment. Quasi-experimental studies, according to Cook and Campbell, are those that "have treatments, outcome measures, and experimental units, but do not use random assignment to create the comparisons from which treatment-caused change is inferred."[2]

The baseline group in quasi experiments are referred to as *comparison groups* as opposed to control groups. Researchers create or construct comparison groups in various ways. Comparison groups, for example, can be groups of people who are similar to the treatment groups, but are located in other sites, for example, in a different city where the treatment to be tested is not administered. Another approach employs statistical techniques applied to available data sets about people similar to those in the treatment group. This is referred to as the *simulation* or *econometric* method for establishing the counterfactual state.

In some cases, demonstration studies are conducted without either a control group or a comparison group; here the object is to compare the treated group *before and after* they have participated in the tested program or activity. Most social science researchers do not like this approach because it is possible that the presumed effects (the before and after differences in this case) might have occurred in any event, that is, in the absence of the tested treatment. In education and job training programs, for example, what is called "the aging-vat effect" refers to the fact that certain things happen to people (for instance, they work more and earn more) simply because they are getting older. This effect, in research parlance, could "confound" a demonstration study that did not have either a control group or a comparison group. The essential point is that random assignment is preferred by social policy researchers because they believe it is the best basis for *predicting* whether a given tested treatment will work if it is *replicated* or *generalized*, whereas the techniques used in quasi experiments are much less certain.

Two more terms need to be defined, *dependent variables* and *independent variables*. Dependent variables refer to the outcome(s) of the tested treatment. These variables are also called left-hand variables. Independent variables, the right-hand side of the equation, include two main types of variables, the treatment being tested and the characteristics of the people being treated.

This terminology is neither rigid nor absolute. In fact, the term *demonstration research* is not universally used in the way I have used it here. I prefer to use *demonstration research* because it is broader and more inclusive than the main alternative, *social experiment*. For most people interested in social policy and social policy research, *demonstration* refers to studies that use a variety of different techniques, including random assignment, to establish the counterfactual state, whereas *social experiment* tends to be reserved for studies based on random assignment.

I have another reason for this preferred terminology. *Social experiment*, when applied to studies that use people as research objects, raises politically controversial concerns about using human beings as guinea pigs. A body of principles and rules of practice under the heading of the "treatment of human subjects" defines acceptable ways of treating people who participate in research projects. These important standards should be adhered to. However, as a tactical matter in discussions of applied social science research, there is an advantage in using the broader and less controversial term *demonstration research*, assuming of course that we deal satisfactorily with the issue of human subject treatment when it arises.

Negative Income Tax Demonstrations

The first and most famous large-scale demonstration research project in the field of social policy in the United States that used random assignment was the New Jersey negative income tax study. The aim of the negative income tax as an approach to welfare reform is to encourage able-bodied, working-age welfare recipients to enter the labor force and ultimately to become self-supporting. The most important operational feature of the negative income tax is that able-bodied, working-age adults with children receive welfare cash-assistance payments on a basis that provides an incentive to work. Under such a scheme, recipients who work are allowed to retain some proportion of their earnings. The rate at which their earnings are "taxed" (that is, reducing their welfare benefits for some part of each dollar earned) is called the "negative income tax rate" or "welfare reduction rate."

The negative income tax experiments were initiated under President Johnson. The main proponents of the negative income tax, who originally sought to have this idea adopted as part of Johnson's "war on poverty," were liberal economists both inside and outside government, including James Tobin, Robert Lampman, Joseph Pechman, Joseph Kershaw, and Robert Levine. Levine, who was head of research in the Office of Economic Opportunity (OEO) during this period, recalls that a negative income tax plan was proposed to the White

House in September 1965, but was "never taken seriously by the Johnson administration."[3]

The most widely discussed issue raised by the proposals for a negative income tax involved the work-incentive effect of subsidies to able-bodied, working-age adults. Would a negative income tax increase or undermine the work incentives of recipients? Proponents of a negative income tax argued that it would increase work incentives and work effort because recipients would be better off if they worked; their total income (earnings plus income support) would rise as their earnings increased.

Another salient point about the labor market effects of a negative income tax should be explained here. Most negative income tax proposals would add people to the welfare rolls in introducing the work-incentive feature of such a plan. The work-incentive issue now comes into sharper focus. It may be that for people already on the welfare rolls a negative income tax increases their work effort, but for the people added to the rolls, which could be an even larger group, work incentive will be reduced because they now need not work as hard to receive their current level of income. The key question involves the *net* effect. In the aggregate, will people work more or less because of the introduction of a negative income tax?

As indicated, the negative income tax experiments represented a fallback position for the supporters of this approach to welfare reform. Rather than jettisoning this idea altogether when Lyndon Johnson refused to consider it, supporters of the negative income tax saw a demonstration study as a way to keep it on the policy agenda. Officials of the Office of Economic Opportunity (the lead agency in Johnson's war on poverty) adopted a proposal by Heather Ross, then a doctoral student working for the Council of Economic Advisors, to conduct a demonstration research project with random assignment on the negative income tax concept. The OEO contracted with the Institute for Poverty Research at the University of Wisconsin in Madison and Mathematica Policy Research of Princeton, New Jersey, to design the experiment. Economists at Princeton University's Industrial Relations Section, working with the staff of Mathematica, also had a major hand in the design and conduct of these experiments.

The role of social scientists in launching the negative income tax experiments raises a thought-provoking question. Some may feel that there is something wrong with a situation in which social scientists conduct research to advance a policy objective they themselves favor. Although I do not think this is a problem, an important caveat needs to be entered. This position that social scientists can legitimately conduct demonstration research to test ideas that they personally favor is much easier to defend if the research project uses *random assignment.* Random assignment reduces the problem of bias toward the tested plan on the part of both the researchers and the sponsors of a demonstration research project.

A negative income tax scheme can be thought of as having a number of movable parts. The design of a specific plan involves arranging these parts in a way that maximizes the objectives of policymakers. Policymakers are likely, for example, to want to (1) establish what they regard as an adequate level of support for recipients; (2) provide a strong work incentive for the people receiving benefits; and (3) avoid having their plan involve what would be regarded as excessive costs. The two main movable parts in determining how these objectives can be achieved are the benefit level and the tax rate. Holding costs constant, policymakers playing the negative income tax game select some combination of a basic benefit level and a tax rate that dictates the "break-even point," the point at which a person's benefits under the terms of a particular negative income tax plan are reduced to zero.

Overall, the income-incidence pattern of the U.S. population is diamond-shaped. There are relatively much smaller numbers of people in the very bottom and top income groups. The largest numbers of people are in the middle-income ranges. Hence, as the coverage of a negative income tax plan increases up the income ladder into the middle-income ranges, the number of people affected also increases. The working poor added to welfare rolls under a negative income tax plan receive a smaller benefit than people who are very poor (those who have no income and would be covered by virtually any type of welfare program), but the number of people involved is larger than the former group. The higher the break-even point of a negative income tax scheme—that is, the point at which working poor people receive zero benefits—the greater will be the problem for politicians that the net overall cost of their plan may make it difficult to enact. The common response of politicians is to compromise. They may, for example, decide to lower the basic benefit or raise the tax rate in order to fit their plan to a particular budget parameter that is regarded as acceptable. This inexorable arithmetic can produce a conundrum. Designers of negative income tax plans have likened the experience to trying to compress a balloon; if you push air out of one area it goes into another. Each time a compromise is made, the argument for the basic idea of the negative income tax is weakened.

In the mid-1960s when the negative income tax experiments were being developed, and as these aspects of the negative income tax idea became increasingly apparent, concerns about the impact of a negative income tax expanding the rolls and raising the costs of welfare gave some political leaders cold feet about even testing the negative income tax concept. When the time came to announce the start of the demonstration planned for New Jersey, officials of the Office of Economic Opportunity hesitated. The director of the OEO at the time was Sargent Shriver, former head of the Peace Corps. Despite this initial hesitation, Shriver decided to proceed, but to do so on a low-key basis. The contract for the first phase of the work on the

New Jersey experiment was paid out of previously appropriated funds, and its announcement was withheld until after Congress had recessed for Labor Day in 1967. In recognition of the potential political pitfalls, Shriver's aides convinced him to change the name of the program from negative income tax to the "work incentives" program.[4] The new name, however, never took hold.

The first payments in the New Jersey negative income tax demonstration were made in Trenton, New Jersey, in 1968. This demonstration, which also included other New Jersey cities and Scranton, Pennsylvania, focused on two-parent welfare families. Altogether, the demonstration had a total sample of 1,350 families in the treatment and the control groups. The families in the treatment group received varying levels of negative income tax payments combined with varying rates of tax applied to the earnings they received from work. Eight negative income tax plans were tested with ranges of the basic income guarantee from 50 percent to 125 percent of the poverty line and with three tax rates, 30 percent, 50 percent, and 70 percent.[5] The experiment lasted three years.

This capsule description does not begin to do justice to the complexity of the task of mounting this first income-maintenance experiment. One year into the work New Jersey introduced a welfare plan on a statewide basis that aided two-parent welfare families on a more generous basis than several of the tested negative income tax plans. As a result, a new negative income tax plan with a higher benefit level had to be instituted. A dispute about this change between the University of Wisconsin Institute for Poverty Research (which was responsible for designing the New Jersey study) and Mathematica (which had the operations contract for this study) became so intense that at the last minute the dispute was assigned to an outside expert, James Tobin, a professor of economics at Yale University, for arbitration.[6]

Due to these and other complications of the New Jersey

study, experts at the Department of Health, Education, and Welfare (which inherited the responsibility for the negative income tax experiments from the Office of Economic Opportunity in the Nixon years) took the position that results from the New Jersey demonstrations should not be used for policy purposes. Instead, they said major policy reliance should be placed on the results from the larger successor negative income tax experiments designed during the execution phase of the New Jersey study. These successor negative income tax demonstrations were conducted in two cities, Seattle and Denver, and in a number of smaller rural communities in three states— Indiana, Iowa, and North Carolina. Initially, the main urban portion of this next round of negative income tax experiments was planned for only one city, Seattle, but a sharp decline in Washington State's volatile economy led to the decision to add Denver as a major urban site. This research is known as the SIME/DIME experiment. The "IME" portion of this acronym stands for income-maintenance experiment, the "S" for Seattle and the "D" for Denver. Operations for this next series of negative income tax experiments began in 1970. Eventually, they included 4,800 families, both intact and single-parent families in rural and urban sites.

As it turned out, the idea of a negative income tax as tested in both the New Jersey and SIME/DIME studies seeped into the policy process well before the results of the experiments were available. Welfare expert Gilbert Y. Steiner characterizes this history as one of "research following reality."[7] Nixon's welfare reform plan, called the Family Assistance Plan or FAP, was announced in 1969, just as the first payments were being made in the New Jersey and Pennsylvania demonstrations. Nixon's plan embodied the idea of the negative income tax. It was heavily influenced by policy analysts in the government, many of whom had a hand in the design and execution of both the New Jersey and SIME/DIME experiments.

As a federal government official during this period (assistant director of the Office of Management and Budget and later deputy undersecretary of Health, Education, and Welfare), I was involved in the development of Nixon's proposals for welfare reform. I have since come to view Nixon's FAP, grounded as it was in the concept of the negative income tax, as the wrong road to welfare reform, but at the time I was an advocate of the plan. For purposes of this chapter, the most interesting subject is the role the results of the negative income tax demonstrations played in the debates in Congress on welfare reform.

Nixon's Family Assistance Plan passed the House twice under the leadership of the Ways and Means Committee Chairman Wilbur Mills, but FAP came under heavy fire in the Senate. Several senators, notably Finance Committee Chairman Russell Long and John Williams of Delaware (the ranking minority member of the committee), attacked the plan on the grounds that it would undermine, rather than enhance, work incentives. Under the pressure of these attacks, officials in the Office of Economic Opportunity released "preliminary" results of the New Jersey demonstration in February 1970. These preliminary findings indicated no adverse effects on work effort under the New Jersey negative income tax experiments. The OEO report went so far as to state that there was, "in fact, a slight indication that the participants' overall work effort actually increased during the initial test period." Senator Williams, a strong opponent of the Nixon Family Assistance Plan, was highly skeptical of this report. He questioned both its veracity and timing and called upon the General Accounting Office (an arm of the Congress) to review the OEO findings. The General Accounting Office responded that the report on the New Jersey study was "premature."[8]

It is unlikely that the controversy over the early release of the New Jersey findings had an effect on the chances for passage of Nixon's Family Assistance Plan; it was already in deep trouble. However, it certainly did not help matters in terms of the hopes of proponents of demonstration research.

A similar political backfire occurred later over the results of the Seattle-Denver income-maintenance demonstration. By now, a coterie of people had accrued long experience with a number of welfare reform efforts and negative income tax experiments. In particular, Daniel Patrick Moynihan's role reflects the rise and fall of the negative income tax idea. Moynihan was a senior advisor in the White House during Nixon's first term. Despite the fact that in his prior government service in the Kennedy and Johnson administrations and as a professor at Harvard he had been a proponent of children's allowance (rather than a negative income tax) as the best road to welfare reform, Moynihan became an influential advocate of the negative income tax approach to welfare reform as encompassed in Nixon's FAP.* He teamed up with the secretary of Health, Education, and Welfare and long-time Nixon aide Robert Finch to convince Nixon that this plan, largely drafted by holdovers from the Johnson administration, was the best available and most dramatic approach for overhauling the welfare system.

In this period, concern was widespread about problems of the welfare system—rapidly rising costs and caseloads, and great disparities in benefit levels among the states, with very low benefits in some states. Many believed that welfare encouraged families to break up or never form, and that it discouraged work effort. Vincent J. and Vee Burke, in their influential book on Nixon's Family Assistance Plan, emphasize the part played by growing welfare roles in getting this issue, "typically shunned by the White House," on the Nixon agenda. "In the decade of the 1960s the proportion of children on relief more

---

*Children's allowances are paid to all families with children according to the number of children and without regard to income. Many European countries have such schemes with recoupment for higher-income families achieved through the tax system.

than doubled from 3.5 percent of those under eighteen in 1960 to 6.8 percent in 1969 and 8.7 percent in 1970. The welfare explosion angered taxpayers and put severe pressure upon state treasuries, especially in such states as Illinois, California, Pennsylvania, and New York."[9] Nixon, who also saw welfare reform as an important opportunity for his administration to surprise and outmaneuver liberals on social policy issues, was especially influenced by Moynihan, whose knowledge of the subject was extensive and whose winning personality and knack for a turn of phrase greatly appealed to Nixon.

This was 1969. As already mentioned, the New Jersey negative income tax experiments were barely under way. The results of the New Jersey experiments would not appear for another four years, and it would not be until well into the Carter administration before the Seattle-Denver results would be available.

By 1978, when the results of the Seattle-Denver negative income tax demonstrations did become available, the game and the roles of many of the players had changed. In particular, Moynihan, always a leader in this field, was now a U.S. Senator and chairman of the welfare subcommittee of the Senate Finance Committee in 1978. In this capacity, he used his subcommittee skillfully as a forum to examine the results of the SIME/DIME research. The hearing record makes interesting reading. Moynihan was the only senator in attendance. His exchanges with witnesses (most of whom were social scientists in fields closely related to Moynihan's) resembled a graduate seminar in social science more than a congressional hearing. The main theme that emerged in this postmortem on the experiments was that the results undercut the basic idea of a negative income tax. At the hearings, researchers disagreed about the seriousness of the problems indicated by the SIME/DIME results, chiefly according to their political orientation. Liberals in the research community acknowledged that the findings undercut the case for a negative income tax, but tended to downplay the magnitude of these adverse effects. On the other hand, conservatives in the research community were almost gleeful in their use of the findings of the research to show the futility of the idea of a negative income tax.

Moynihan, in an interesting way, was in the middle. He originally supported the idea of a negative income tax, but in the end he sided with the conservatives in his assessment of the implications for social policy of the findings from the negative income tax experiments. Writing to William F. Buckley in 1978, he said, "We were wrong about a guaranteed income. Seemingly, it is calamitous."[10]

The results of the experiments went against the arguments of the proponents of the negative income tax in two ways. The tested payment schemes resulted in reduced earnings and hours of work for recipients. They also appeared to have an adverse effect on families by encouraging family breakup rather than enhancing family stability as was claimed would be the case.

In November 1978, when Moynihan held the second of his two hearings on the experiments, Robert Spiegelman, director of the Seattle-Denver research for the Stanford Research Institute, presented dramatic testimony on the adverse effects of these experiments on family stability. This report on the SIME/DIME study also showed that the tested negative income tax plans caused substantial reductions in labor activity for persons enrolled in the relatively longer-term plans and for women. Gary Burtless and Robert Haveman, in summarizing these results, said that "prime-aged men reduced their annual hours of work by 9 or 10 percent; and that their spouses reduced annual hours by 17 to 20 percent; and that women heading single-parent families reduced annual hours by more than 20 percent—perhaps as much as 28 to 32 percent." These findings were published at the time officials in the Carter administration were putting together Carter's welfare reform legislation, which like Nixon's had the basic features of a negative income tax. The immediate result was a decision to trim back the Carter plan, because the research results increased the cost estimates for the benefit schedule in the Carter proposal.[11]

Moynihan's view of these events is contained in a book on social policy published eight years after these hearings in 1986. In the book, he was especially critical of Carter's secretary of Health, Education, and Welfare, Joseph Califano, for his failure to present an assessment on the adverse effects of the SIME/DIME demonstration on family stability, calling his behavior "inexcusable."[12] Among experts in the field, there is now considerable controversy about these findings; new interpretations challenge the earlier Stanford Research Institute reports on the adverse effects of the SIME/DIME demonstrations on family stability.[13]

The most interesting insight in Moynihan's postmortem is his view of the testimony of Stanford University economist John Cogan. Cogan, a conservative, testified at the Moynihan hearings in 1978 about his reanalysis of the New Jersey results, which showed much larger reductions in employment and earnings than those reported by the researchers who conducted this experiment. His results suggested a work-withdrawal effect as much as four times greater than that reported. Cogan's methodology is not easily explained and has been debated by researchers. To summarize, Cogan divided the treatment group according to whether people did or did not participate in the demonstration. In the case of the controls, he divided them in a similar way according to whether the members of the control group did or did not receive welfare benefits. Although many social scientists objected to Cogan's methodology, it is notable that Moynihan did not. At the hearing in 1978 he expressed incredulity in response to Cogan's findings. Moynihan said that the earlier reports on the New Jersey study were "bordering on malpractice" in light of Cogan's testimony.[14] He asked for, and received, agency comments on Cogan's work, and agency officials believed, at least this is what they told me, that Moynihan later accepted their reasoning as to why Cogan's reanalysis was flawed. The record, however, is different from what the agency officials claimed. Moynihan, in his 1986 retrospective, described Cogan's testimony favorably. "The subcommittee, which is to say the general public, learned nothing until one afternoon in November 1978 when John Cogan, a young economist from Stanford, came to testify and told us, 'They won't tell you this, but it hasn't worked.' "[15]

The little drama was complete. The high hopes of supporters of demonstration research in this case failed to materialize. As discussed in the previous chapter, Henry Aaron was right. The effects of the negative income tax demonstrations were perverse from the point of view of supporters of comprehensive welfare reform plans along the lines proposed by Presidents Nixon and Carter.

Discussion

I believe that the negative income tax demonstrations were moderately successful as research projects. They were much less successful, however, as an aid to policymaking. Their results came very late in the policy process, and were ambiguous to say the least. The experiments should not necessarily be faulted for this second reason. The purpose of research is to answer questions honestly and objectively. Moynihan put it very well. In an exchange with Spiegelman of the Stanford Research Institute at the September 1978 hearings on the findings of the negative income tax experiments, he said: "The bringing of systematic inquiry to bear on social issues is not an easy thing. There is no guarantee of pleasant and simple answers, but if you make a commitment to an experimental mode it seems to me—I am not enjoying this hearing one damn bit, but if you make a commitment to an experimental mode, something larger is at stake when you begin to have to deal with the results."[16]

At its roots, the reason for the basically negative findings for the idea of a negative income tax involves the inexorable political arithmetic of this approach to welfare reform. The cost of covering millions of additional people under a negative income tax presented a policy choice that simply was not in the cards in the 1970s. Taking into account the underlying aims of the sponsors of this research, I believe that their research agenda was out of line with the nation's political and social values.

Policy researchers have done a great deal of soul-searching in analyzing the negative income tax demonstrations. Was this trip (that is, this research) necessary? Having participated in the appraisal of this research and having been a participant in decisions about some of the work done on these research projects, I have come to the conclusion that it was not. As I see it, the value of demonstration research in the field of social policy is very much a function of the *types* of programs studied. The key distinction is between income-maintenance and service-type programs. I have major reservations about the usefulness of demonstration research projects to test universal income-maintenance programs such as the negative income tax where the establishment of such a program would be highly visible. After a national debate on this kind of a basic policy change under conditions in which it is widely known that the "rules of the game" have been changed because of a new program that has been adopted, we have reason to expect that the people exposed to this new policy would change their behavior in ways that could not be known in a research environment in which such a debate had not taken place. On the other hand, service-type interventions can be focused on specific programs and places in a much less intrusive way. A new service program, whether job training, child care, or home care for the aged, is likely to be viewed as "just another program" with relatively few people being conscious of the fact that it is structured as a demonstration study.

I also fault the negative income tax experiments for the political reason that they reflected the agenda of researchers and not of politicians. Demonstration studies are expensive and time-consuming. They should only be undertaken in situations in which these *three conditions* apply: (1) politicians are genuinely interested in the program to be tested; (2) they are uncertain as to how it will work; and (3) they are willing to wait for the results of a demonstration study. It is my conclusion, admittedly long after the fact, that the negative income tax experiments did not satisfy these three conditions. To the credit of many of the researchers involved, it was shown on the basis of these experiments that it is possible in the United States to conduct large-scale, rigorous demonstration research projects with random assignment. For the future, however, a different approach to demonstration research is needed in terms of the types of studies conducted.

Another important lesson of the negative income tax demonstrations relates to the disciplinary scope of the research agenda. At a 1974 conference at the Brookings Institution after the New Jersey negative income tax experiments were completed, sociologist Peter Rossi said it was "paradoxical" that despite the heavy reliance of sociologists on primary data collection and the extensive use by psychologists of experimental designs, it was economists who "played the major role in designing and fielding the income maintenance experiments."[17] In a similar vein, sociologist Lee Rainwater complained that what was learned about social behavior in the negative income tax experiments was "remarkably skimpy."[18] In a paper for a 1986 conference on the lessons of this research, Rainwater pointed out that more qualitative data were needed about the people in the experiment and their lives.

The challenge, as I see it, is to devise ways to incorporate other variables—psychological, social, and political—in demonstration research. In my view this is the most important challenge of the future for the effective conduct of both demonstration and evaluation research. Among the kinds of questions one would like to have considered in the case of the negative income tax were these: What is the effect of such a new scheme on people's feelings of self-worth and achievement? What are its effects on children, on families, on communities with a high concentration of dependent welfare families, on state and local governments and other social programs and agencies, and on the larger society? I realize that not all of these questions can necessarily or easily be taken into account. Yet these kinds of questions are basic to this book's argument about the missing links between social science disciplines in the conduct of applied social science research. If we leave out disciplines in demonstration research, we may be neglecting variables in the research equation that are often of critical importance to policymakers.

Other Income-Maintenance Demonstrations

The negative income tax studies are the most famous demonstrations of income-maintenance programs, but they are not the only ones. Other demonstration studies have been conducted in the income-maintenance field in the United States since the New Jersey flagship study was launched. These research projects (some of them very large) were initiated, and much of this research was conducted, under the Nixon and Ford administrations. Some analysts of this period see these demonstrations as a cover for not acting on social issues; however, as stated earlier, there are good reasons to question this interpretation. Besides the negative income tax demonstrations, income-maintenance experiments have been conducted to test housing allowances (vouchers to poor people to change their demand for housing), health insurance for low-income families and individuals, and education vouchers. By far the largest of these demonstrations were the housing voucher demonstrations.

The Housing and Urban Development Act of 1970 authorized funds to test alternative approaches to convert the existing production-focused housing programs of the federal government into housing allowances. The idea of a housing allowance is to influence the demand for housing by providing low-income persons allowances to increase their purchasing power in the housing market. Previous programs supported the construction of low-income housing, thereby stimulating the supply, rather than the demand side, of the housing market. Three housing allowance demonstrations were conducted. The first was a demand demonstration in two sites (the Pittsburgh and Phoenix metropolitan areas) which studied how families would respond to housing allowances; the second demonstration was conducted in two smaller metropolitan areas to assess the effects of housing allowances on housing markets; and the third was an administrative agency demonstration to collect information about the management of housing allowances.[19] The field operations for these demonstrations were carried out in the mid-1970s. The largest demonstration in terms of the number of participants was the housing-market demonstration conducted by the Rand Corporation that included 9,700 households. The Pittsburgh and Phoenix demand demonstration, conducted by Abt Associates of Cambridge, Massachusetts, included approximately 2,500 households and 1,000 controls. Altogether $160 million was spent on these three studies.

Half of the funds were used to pay for the tested programs, and half for data collection and other research operations. Some features of the housing allowance approach have influenced housing policy since these demonstrations were conducted. However, a number of issues raised by the demonstrations have not been resolved, and considerable debate exists within the policy research fraternity about the design and usefulness of these demonstrations.

Another demonstration, which began in 1974, was linked to proposals Presidents Nixon and Ford advanced to establish a new national health insurance system. The aim of this demonstration was to answer questions that could not be "reliably resolved through analysis of non-experimental data."[20] This demonstration, conducted in six sites over an eight-year period (November 1974 to January 1982), enrolled more than 7,000 people in 2,756 families. The research, conducted by the Rand Corporation, tested a range of health insurance programs to determine the effects of different benefit structures and financial features on the utilization of health services, the health status of the participants, and the type and quality of the care they received.[21] The health insurance demonstrations were narrow-gauged. In addition to the kinds of basic issues indicated earlier in the discussion of the negative income tax experiments, some have questioned whether the tested treatments were large enough and discrete enough to serve as a basis for making choices about major policy alternatives.

Another area in which a demonstration studied an income-transfer program—the test of education vouchers—is in many ways the most interesting and also the most seriously flawed of the studies in this category. This demonstration, too, emerged not under Johnson but in the Nixon years to test a favorite idea of University of Chicago economist Milton Friedman. He believes that the government should promote competition in the field of elementary and secondary education by having families receive a voucher they can use to purchase educational services for their children. The demonstration, funded initially by the Office of Economic Opportunity and later by the National Institute for Education, was developed by the Harvard University Center for the Study of Public Policy and was conducted, as in the case of the health insurance demonstration, by the Rand Corporation.[22] Although six school districts initially came forward as candidates to participate in the demonstration, three of them dropped out. As it turned out, only one school district (Alum Rock in San Jose, California) received funds. The Alum Rock school-voucher demonstration lasted five years and cost $9 million. The story is long and complicated, but the plot is clear: just about everything that could go wrong did go wrong. Not only did the project narrow down to one school district, but the state of California failed to pass the necessary enabling legislation, teachers and parents resisted essential features of the voucher plan, and parents were confused by what in the final analysis turned out to be a program with limited variation between the conventional and "new" approaches.

Demonstrations of Service Programs

The other major category of demonstration research is the study of service-type programs. Overall, less activity has taken place under this heading, if we measure activity by the amount of money allocated for such studies, but more individual projects have been done. Some of these studies predate the New Jersey negative income tax study, although the major interest in demonstration research on the part of the research community began in New Jersey.

In the education field, the best-known project that predated the New Jersey negative income tax experiments was the Perry preschool demonstration in Ypsilanti, Michigan, initiated in 1962.[23] Educational psychologists in earlier periods conducted school experiments with random assignment; most of them focused on curriculum changes in a classroom setting with schools or classes as the units of analysis.[24] Although the sample for the Perry preschool demonstration was small (123 black youths at risk of failing school), it used a research design with random assignment. The appreciable benefits of this program over a long period of time (through age nineteen in the fourth phase of this study as reported in 1984) have been widely cited in the literature on preschool education.

For the consideration of service-type demonstration studies in this book, I rely heavily in the chapters that follow on the experience of the demonstrations I know best, studies conducted by the Manpower Demonstration Research Corporation. This corporation was founded in 1974 to conduct the national supported-work demonstration, which was funded by a consortium of federal agencies and the Ford Foundation. Supported work is a treatment model developed by the Vera Institute of Justice in New York City in the late 1960s. It focused on criminal–justice system offenders. As an alternative to incarceration, supported work involved groups of former offenders working together; the aim was to prepare them to obtain and hold regular jobs. Participants worked in paid transitional jobs, typically lasting twelve to eighteen months. Gradually, the support provided to participants was reduced until workers could maintain their own regular employment. In 1974 the Ford Foundation, with major support from the U.S. Department of Labor, decided to test this program outside of New York City and for other groups in addition to former offenders. The three other groups were female welfare family heads; former addicts eighteen years or older enrolled in a drug treatment program currently or in the last six months; and youths aged seventeen to twenty with no high school or equivalency degree and not in school in the last six months. The success of this demonstration led the Manpower Demonstration Research Corporation to undertake a number of other demonstration research studies concerning employment and training services for disadvantaged groups.

The chapters on demonstration research that follow have two purposes. One is to examine in greater detail the problems involved in conducting demonstration studies. Chapter 4 discusses eight obstacles to demonstration research. Chapter 5 describes two research projects undertaken by the Manpower Demonstration Research Corporation in the form of case studies. Both studies—the supported-work and work/welfare demonstration research projects—are related, as are the negative income tax experiments, to the issue of welfare reform, which has been so central to social policy debates in the United States since the 1960s.

4

The Hurdles of
Demonstration Research

THIS CHAPTER CONSIDERS eight major hurdles that must be cleared in testing possible new approaches to the solution of public problems. They involve (1) selection bias; (2) the null hypothesis; (3) contamination; (4) relations with program operators; (5) the quality and consistency of the treatment being tested; (6) the cost and quality of the data used in demonstration studies; (7) the treatment of human subjects in these studies; and (8) the uncertainty of cost-benefit analysis as the final step in the demonstration-research process. Taken together, these eight topics indicate the range of scientific and operational decisions involved in selecting the subjects for demonstration research, developing the design to be used, and executing such studies.

Selection Bias

Selection bias is crucial in determining the *counterfactual state,* the baseline for comparison in a demonstration study. We want to compare the effects of a given tested treatment in a demonstration study to the counterfactual state (the situation that would have existed without the treatment) in order to answer our main research questions: Did the tested treatment make a difference? What kind of a difference did it make, and what was the magnitude of difference? An example will help to explain the research challenge posed by the problem of selection bias.

The example involves state education officials who are considering ways to improve the reading proficiency of junior high school students with reading problems. Assume that a computer-assisted remedial reading program, which seemed to many observers to be successful, has been sponsored by a state government in a particular junior high school. The question is whether it should be extended to other schools. State school officials want to compare the reading scores of the participants with the scores of students who are not in the special reading remediation program. But how should they do this? One way is to compare the observed increases in the reading scores of the students in the computer-assisted model reading program with the average change in reading scores for all junior high school students in a particular school district in which the model program was conducted. But this may not be a good basis of comparison from the point of view of the proponents of the program who want it to be extended as a way to help other junior high school students with reading problems.

Let us assume that we have reading scores for all of the students in the model reading program and for all junior high school students in the school district in which it was conducted for the same time period. These scores show that the average increase in reading scores for all students was 105 percent of some standard of achievement compared to 78 percent for the students in the model reading program. If the school officials doing the analysis are sympathetic to the program, as is often the case, they may reject the "normal" 105 percent achievement standard as the basis for comparison. They may argue, for example, that one should compare the results of the special reading program with what happens to other students *who have problems*. Our baseline, according to this view, should be other students who need this kind of special help. But how do we find a group with the same problems as the students in the special program? And, even if we could find such a group, would this be a satisfactory basis for comparison?

Let us stipulate further that the model reading remediation program was offered to all students with reading proficiency scores below a certain level in the schools in which it was conducted. Some students applied for the program. Some did not. Maybe what really made a difference was the act of applying, that is, the motivation of the students who came forward because they wanted this special help. If we compare the reading scores of students in the program with the scores of apparently similar students who were not in the program, we may find a positive impact, but actually it may be the impact of this "M factor" of motivation.

The point is not that motivation may have made the difference, *but that we do not know what made the difference.* This is what is involved in the idea of selection bias—the possibility that the results of a given demonstration were biased because the people selected for the tested program were different from the controls for some reason (conscious or unconscious, deliberate or accidental) having to do with the way in which they were selected. This is where random assignment has its great strength. If we had tested the reading remediation program systematically on a random-assignment basis, we would be in a much better position (not perfect, but much better) to say what difference the model program made, using standard statistical procedures. In effect, under these conditions we assume that because we used random assignment we are able to control for any bias that could have occurred either on the part of teachers or parents in selecting students who otherwise meet the program eligibility standards. This applies either to a deliberate bias (for example, teachers may select the best or worst students) or to our M factor (students who apply are personally motivated). In a similar way, the key could be an "F factor," in which students who come forward for the program have a home environment in which family encouragement reinforces or has more impact than the special program in reading remediation. Random assignment solves the problems of M factors and F factors, and X and Y factors, because it creates conditions under which, if our sample is large enough and properly drawn, there is just as much chance that an M- or F-factor person would be in the treatment group as in the control group.

Researchers can use statistical procedures to attempt to control for selection bias when random assignment is not used, but the view of most researchers is that these alternative techniques are inferior to random assignment. Some researchers even argue that they are unacceptable. In short, there is little dispute among researchers that random assignment is the best way to deal with the problem of selection bias. A key question is whether we can find acceptable alternatives when for some reason (relating to the cost, feasibility, the time frame, or the ethics of a given demonstration research setting) random assignment is inappropriate or not possible.

The experience of the Manpower Demonstration Research Corporation (MDRC) is relevant here. The most striking finding from the national supported-work demonstration described in the previous chapter was that this program showed positive results for two participant groups. (All of the participants in each of the four target groups in this study were randomly assigned to a treatment group or a control group.) The results of the supported-work demonstration were by far strongest for one group—female family heads on welfare. This finding was used in an ingenious way by one researcher to study the role of random assignment in demonstration research.

Using data from MDRC's supported-work demonstration, Robert J. LaLonde studied the question of whether another research approach (that is, other than random assignment) could have been used to replicate the supported-work control group. Specifically, if LaLonde could use conventional econometric techniques to identify a comparison group that was just like the supported-work control group, or very similar to it, then the researchers in this case could have saved themselves a lot of trouble. They could have used statistical techniques to create a comparison group. Then they could have measured the impact of the supported-work program by comparing the outcome (dependent) variables for the people in the supported-work program to data about the same characteristics for the people in the statistically simulated comparison group. According to LaLonde, when researchers do not have a randomly selected control group, "an econometrician must first select a group of individuals from the population to serve as a comparison group and then specify an econometric model that accounts both for the difference in earnings between the treatment and the comparison groups and for the treatments' decision to participate in training. . . . MDRC's experimental data offer labor economists an opportunity to test the non-experimental methods of program evaluation."[1]

LaLonde used standard econometric techniques applied to data from the University of Michigan's Panel Study on Income Dynamics, data on earnings and other demographic characteristics from the Current Population Survey conducted by the Bureau of the Census, and data from the Social Security Administration to determine the earnings of a group of people like those in the supported-work program. In this way he simulated the counterfactual state; and he asked, "Would it be like the situation for the control group in MDRC's supported-work demonstration?"

The short answer to LaLonde's query was that his experiment on experimentation did not work. Said LaLonde: "The econometric models used to evaluate training programs generate imprecise estimates of training effects. This imprecision underscores the importance of a classical experimental design both to the evaluation of the national supported work program and perhaps other programs as well. Without random assignment an econometrician faces a considerable range of training effects; it is unlikely he will choose the correct one."[2]

Based on LaLonde's work with MDRC data tapes, the supported-work demonstration showed net additional earnings of $851 per year for female family heads on welfare. LaLonde compared this outcome with the earnings experience of four different simulated comparison groups of poor women. One of his four results was close to the findings from the MDRC study; it showed a net gain for program participants of $1,090. A second simulation was also positive, but exaggerated the benefits of supported work, showing an earnings gain of over $3,000. Two other simulations showed negative results. The women in these simulated comparison groups earned less than participants in the supported-work demonstration. In one case the earnings difference was $2,822, in the other $3,357. The clinching argument for LaLonde on the importance of random assignment in demonstration research was that he could find no basis on which researchers would have known how to select the comparison group from among these and other possible simulated comparison groups.

Labor economist Orley Ashenfelter, head of the Princeton University Industrial Relations Section, said about LaLonde's study, "The evaluation of the economic benefits of training programs will be greatly enhanced by the use of classical experimental methods. . . . much of the non-experimental estimation of the effects of training programs seems dependent on elements of model specification that cannot be subjected to powerful statistical tests. . . . In sum, it appears that in the area of analysis of training programs the econometric methods available may not be able to deliver the benefits that randomized trials offer."[3]

The work by LaLonde stimulated other researchers to examine this basic question involving the reliability of alternatives to random assignment as a research method to assess the impact of employment and training programs. Rebecca Maynard at Mathematica Policy Research joined this group, coauthoring an article with LaLonde supporting his skeptical view of the value of alternative methodologies. An entire issue of the journal *Evaluation Review* (August 1987) was devoted to this subject; it includes the LaLonde-Maynard article. It also includes a contrary view put forward by James J. Heckman. Heckman's article, written with his associates at the University of Chicago, expresses the belief that "reliable nonexperimental evaluation methods can and will be developed in the future for all subsidized employment and training programs."[4]

My own view is that in some circumstances we should use research methods other than random assignment because of feasibility or ethical considerations, and in other situations simply because the costs of random assignment would be too high. Still, as a general rule, I believe that random assignment should be the preferred core methodology for demonstration research, especially when the terrain is unfamiliar or the treatments being tested are new and especially important. There are both political and substantive reasons for this conclusion.

It has already been observed that social scientists who conduct demonstration research in the field of social policy often study programs they themselves favor as a means to achieve policy goals they care about. One can think of this as an issue of selection bias on the part of the research community. Researchers are often biased in favor of the idea that government can do things to solve problems. *They believe in government.* An effective way to deal with this problem of program selection bias on the part of the researchers is to use random assignment. Once researchers have designed a demonstration research project using random assignment, it limits conscious or unconscious manipulation of their data. Random assignment in these terms can be said to keep the research process honest. This enhances the credibility of demonstration research in the field of social policy.

But random assignment is not the only way to conduct demonstration research. Some demonstration studies use other approaches. For example, one can compare people in other and similar places to those in places in which a demonstration is carried out. This is the "comparison site" approach. People in the comparison site are matched to the people in the treatment group. In other studies, people who fit the eligibility standards of a particular program but did not participate in it are used as the comparison group. They may, for example, have been applicants who initially came forward but did not apply or for whom space was not available. In other studies, econometric techniques applied to existing data sets are used to simulate a control group. Many types of data can be used in this way, some of which, it may be argued, are more appropriate than those that LaLonde used.

All of these alternatives to random assignment raise substantial issues for the conduct of demonstration research. I have listed these alternatives here in the rank order of their relative desirability. The main point is that some of these less-good approaches (that is, not as good as random assignment) are better than others. The selection of a research design depends on a variety of factors. The research hurdle of selection bias is high and crucial. Nevertheless, I do not believe that its importance justifies the position, which unfortunately is widely held among researchers, that there are no acceptable alternatives to random assignment for demonstration research. I have more to say in what follows about other approaches to estimating the counterfactual state. For now, it suffices to say that the problem of selection bias is critical enough to make random assignment the preferred methodology.

The Null Hypothesis

The second hurdle for demonstration research involves the "null hypothesis." This has more to do with the choice of programs to test than with the choice of the method to test them. The idea here is that in the real world in which many factors and forces impinge in rapid-fire fashion on people's lives, the only kind of a program one can test is one that is large enough to make a detectable difference. Researchers refer to this problem as proving the null hypothesis, that is, finding no impact when an impact might actually have occurred.

Again, the supported-work demonstration helps illustrate this point. When MDRC was designing the supported-work demonstration, Robert Lampman, a welfare economist who at the time was a member of the board of the corporation, stressed that the supported-work intervention must be large enough and last long enough so that we could reasonably expect that it would have an impact. In this way, Lampman believed that we would avoid loading the deck in favor of the null hypothesis. "When persons with severe employment handicaps and disabilities are singled out for remediation, positive and lasting effects are not likely. In the case of supported work, the odds in favor of the null hypothesis were even greater . . . since the four groups chosen were from among those least likely to succeed in the labor market."[5]

On the whole, I agree with Lampman and others who favor focusing demonstration research on relatively large interventions that could be expected to affect people's lives in a detectable way. If we are going to go to the trouble of designing and conducting a demonstration research project with random assignment, such studies must be of substantial policy interventions that can reasonably be expected to make a difference in the lives of the people in the treatment group. Nevertheless, it should be noted that a number of the demonstration research projects undertaken by MDRC have detected significant impacts of relatively small and short-term policy interventions.

Contamination

In the application of the scientific method under laboratory conditions, we often hear comments about efforts to avoid contamination. A chemistry or physics experiment may be conducted in an airtight chamber in order to avoid having contaminants in the air spoil the experiment. In demonstration research, we use the word "contamination" in a way that some people may find objectionable. It refers to external factors that affect the treatment or control or comparison group in ways that distort the comparison we seek to make. If, for example, we are testing a program to provide health care for infants, we would on scientific grounds like to have our treatment and control groups be "pure" in the sense that one group gets the treatment and the other does not. But what if we are doing a study on an intensive program of infant health care in a given locale and while the study is under way a local group decides that it should open a new health clinic to provide health care services for infants? If we are using a research design with random assignment, the result might be that the treatment has no or a very small impact because the infants in the control group are receiving services very similar to those provided to the infants in the treatment group. Under such conditions, we are comparing apples with apples. We are comparing the treatment that is the subject of the demonstration with other and perhaps very similar treatments that are provided in the community in which the demonstration is being conducted.

In one of the MDRC studies, this issue came into play in an unanticipated and what turned out to be important way. The case involved Project Redirection, a program to provide integrated counseling and other social services to very young welfare mothers. The treatment group can be thought of as "children with children." The research design in this case was quasi-experimental. The dependent (outcome) variables for the participants in the program were compared with the same characteristics of teens who met the Project Redirection eligibility requirements but lived in areas not offering the Redirection program. What MDRC found in this case was that the impacts of the Redirection program were "mixed but disappointing."[6] One apparent reason for this result was that the people in the comparison sites received services (parenting classes, medical care for the baby, birth control counseling, educational counseling, employment activities) similar to those given to the participants in Project Redirection.

This situation can be referred to as "contamination," although this use of the term is not meant to imply that there is anything wrong about the fact that the provision of services to the members of the comparison group in this case was much higher than had been expected by the planners of the demonstration. In a real sense, this was a *positive* finding of the research.

It should be noted that the contamination problem in this case was not a function of the decision to use comparison sites instead of random assignment. Random assignment was found to be infeasible for political reasons in the case of Project Redirection. The programs in the demonstration were small and MDRC faced concerns on the part of program operators that they did not have a large enough applicant pool to select randomly one out of every two (or some other number) of applicants. Program operators—this subject is discussed next— often have a different point of view than the researchers. In any event, the service contamination that occurred in the case of Project Redirection could just as easily have occurred with a research design using random assignment. For example, other job-assistance programs for welfare mothers operating in the study sites could have reduced the observed treatment effect of the supported-work program.

Relations with Program Operators

Many of the hurdles discussed in this chapter suggest the kinds of delicate research compromises that are necessary because of the complexity of the real world. In the case of the MDRC Project Redirection study, the reason for using the comparison site design (as opposed to random assignment) was that the program operators resisted random assignment. The sponsoring organizations were small and they operated small programs. In discussions with the MDRC staff, program operators indicated that the limited size of the pool of applicants who could be expected to come forward for the program to be tested would not allow them to run a program that required them to turn away the applicants assigned randomly to a control group. It is not unusual for program operators to resist having to randomly assign eligible people to a no-treatment control group.

A major challenge to demonstration researchers under these conditions is to convince the operators of the program to be tested (whether state or local government officials or the heads of nonprofit organizations) that they should participate in research and furthermore that they should employ random assignment. This often requires sensitive negotiations between researchers and potential program operators. Program operators are being asked systematically to reject some eligible applicants who come forward. They often argue that these are *people*, not research objects. This act of turning away people who live in their community (and who may be known personally by program operators) is understandably difficult; sometimes it is seen as unacceptable.

The funders and managers of a demonstration have two main types of leverage under these conditions. One is money. Typically, they pay some portion of the program costs. This may influence program operators to join a demonstration research project. Their reasoning in this case may be that they are getting *something extra* for the people whom they want to serve in a situation in which, in any event, the service involved cannot be provided to all of the people who come forward and are eligible. Hence, the rationing of this service on a random basis is justifiable. One can even argue that random assignment, like a lottery, is actually the fairest method of rationing a service under these conditions, although others, particularly some program operators, may argue that the degree or character of need or commitment (our "M factor") is a better basis on which to select participants.

Another argument that the funders and managers of a demonstration research project can bring to bear in this situation involves the basic case for applied social science research. If the people who provide a particular service can prove that *it works,* then that service may eventually be provided on a broader basis to more people who need it because of the effect that the research findings can be expected to have on policymakers.

Quality and Consistency of Treatment

Once a research topic and design are decided upon and a program sponsor agrees to participate, other critical operational issues may emerge. Consider a case, for example, in which a preschool education program being tested in a demonstration project is not being provided in the way the researchers intended. It may be that staff members of the community group providing the service decided that they did not like the research specifications, or it may be that they simply do not perform well. What is the researcher to do under such conditions?

On a conceptual level, we have what can be called "the repairman's dilemma." Should researchers see to it that the quality of the program is maintained at a high level? Or should they only be concerned about the consistency of the treatment, that is, its consistency with the requirements of the research design? In the former case, researchers would be taking the position that what they are testing is the efficacy of a treatment that is well administered. In the latter case, they would only intervene when the program operator was not using the agreed-upon specifications in providing the tested service.

In another MDRC study, the Youth Incentive Entitlement Pilot Project, this issue arose. This demonstration was mandated by Congress to test saturation programs in selected communities to provide employment to disadvantaged youth, both in school and school dropouts. Over a period of two and a half years, $240 million was spent on this demonstration in seventeen communities in which 76,000 persons were employed as program participants. The U.S. General Accounting Office reported that this demonstration was well managed by MDRC, but that the demonstration was artificial.[7] The MDRC's management oversight was said to be too intrusive. The argument made by the General Accounting Office was that in the conduct of this program, were it to be adopted on a broad basis, the responsible central authorities (the federal government or the states) would not be as demanding or as rigorous in maintaining the quality of the program as was MDRC. My view is that this is one research hurdle (the problem of too high a level of program quality) that we need not worry about. Nevertheless, the experience here points up the challenge of maintaining acceptable—even if not exemplary—standards for the quality and consistency of the treatment in a demonstration study.

Cost and Quality of Data

Almost any large-scale demonstration project is bound to confront appreciable operational problems involving the cost and quality of the data needed to conduct the research. These problems are taken into account here, although this hurdle may be regarded by many social scientists as essentially a managerial issue in demonstration research. Data must be collected in three time periods for both the treatment group and the control or comparison groups in a demonstration study: (1) the baseline at or just before the program starts up; (2) the in-program period (that is, the period during the demonstration); and (3) a postprogram period for data collection. This third period, after the tested treatment is administered, can last a long time—sometimes five to seven years, sometimes longer as in the Perry preschool demonstration described in chapter 3 in which postprogram observations were made over more than a decade. Moreover, the needed data for both program participants and controls often must be obtained from a number of different sources—for example, from program operators and from survey research and governmental records.

Generally, the data-collection tasks associated with a demonstration study are easiest to carry out for people in the treatment group while they are participating in the tested program. But even this can be difficult. Researchers and program operators often do not see eye to eye. Conflicts arise about what program sponsors regard as intrusive data requirements. Even when these issues are resolved, other problems may remain. An example is the requirement, which is frequently included in research protocols, for program sponsors to collect data for the people in the research sample who are selected as program participants even if they do not actually show up and participate in the program being tested.

It is even more difficult to obtain data for participants *after* they leave the program. Program operators usually cannot be enlisted to administer questionnaires. It is often necessary to employ a survey research firm to contact and obtain information from participants in the postprogram period. Such follow-up surveys are expensive, especially if participants have left the community in which the tested program is being conducted. Moreover, if participants cannot be located in the follow-up period, the sample attrition rate can threaten the success of a demonstration study. Considerable resources must be devoted to locating and interviewing participants after they leave a demonstration program.

But all these problems pale in relation to those involved in collecting data on the people in control and comparison groups. For these groups, data are needed for all three time periods—baseline data, information about the experience of these people during the program, and data for a follow-up period of the same duration as that for the participants. Often, the members of control or comparison groups are paid each time they are interviewed, but this is not always enough to overcome the problems of winning their cooperation, especially if the tested treatment is administered to a disadvantaged population.

Overall, the people in both the treatment and control or comparison groups are likely to be highly mobile and hard to locate; they also tend to have limited literacy and verbal skills, which adds to the difficulty of obtaining information about them.

Compromises are often made in the data-collection tasks for demonstration research. Some data elements that are considered desirable are dropped to reduce the time needed to conduct interviews and the cost of interviews. In other cases, the frequency of data collection is sacrificed to cut costs or to limit the intrusiveness of the research process. For the follow-up periods in some studies, public data files are used instead of interviews, in which cases the data may be less complete and accurate than in situations where a survey is administered. Wherever compromises are made, questions arise about the effect such decisions may have on the quality and integrity of the research. These are not the kinds of challenging intellectual questions that fascinate social science researchers. Nevertheless, they are a critical and problematic part of the job of conducting a demonstration study.

Treatment of Human Subjects

As the demonstration research approach gained ground in the late 1960s and 1970s, so did concern about the protection of human subjects in such studies. This concern, as would be expected, was particularly salient for liberals.

In 1974, the Department of Health, Education, and Welfare (HEW) issued regulations that required researchers receiving HEW funds to establish local "institutional review boards" to ensure that demonstration research projects protected the rights of human subjects.[8] At first, the Office of Management and Budget required that these regulations be applied on a governmentwide basis. Later, this policy was changed, and the regulations applied only to demonstrations paid for by HEW or its successor department, the Department of Health and Human Services.

Two central premises are reflected in these rules for dealing with human subjects and in the similar standards developed by other groups. Both are derived from experience in medical research. One premise, grounded in the Hippocratic oath, is that social policy researchers, like medical practitioners who serve as "changers of men," should *do no harm.*[9] They should make certain that no one is harmed by virtue of being a member of a treatment or control group for a demonstration study. The second premise requires "informed consent." This means that the individuals (both participants and the members of a control group) in a demonstration study should be given an explanation of the research process and should be asked to agree to participate in that process. Writing in 1975, P. Michael Timpane and Alice Rivlin commented that "informed consent is by now an entrenched canon of medical experimentation and has been adopted implicitly by most social experimenters."[10] Although few policy researchers quarrel with these two central premises, their implications both for the substance and process of demonstration studies are considerable, especially in the case of demonstrations that have a randomly selected control group.

In 1975, the Brookings Institution held a conference on the ethical and legal issues of social experimentation. The conference raised a number of difficult questions. Can children ever be the subject of a social experiment? Who can give informed consent for them? Their parents? School officials? Some participants ruled out all social experiments involving children and also for other groups for whom it was argued informed consent effectively cannot be obtained, for example, prisoners and mental patients. This view was challenged by other participants at the conference from the social policy research community who saw little risk, only potential gains, for the subjects of social experiments. Other participants from the research community argued that all decisions involving social programs involve risks similar to those of a social experiment, yet we do not require informed consent in every case in which the society intervenes in a life situation.

As noted earlier, the requirement to obtain informed consent in social experiments is now widely and well accepted by researchers. Still, questions of execution—how researchers tell potential participants about a research project and how much they tell them—can introduce problems. Both participants and controls in a demonstration study, for example, may react to an experiment in a way that reflects what they perceive to be the expectations of its sponsors based on what they are told in obtaining their informed consent. Or members of the treatment group may as a group decide to undermine the program for some reason having to do with their attitude toward the researchers, program operators, or social programs generally. In a similar way, members of a randomly selected control group, aware that they are part of "something special" and are being observed, may develop a "show-them" attitude involving a desire to do well in terms of the criteria on which they believe that they are being studied. These kinds of behavior produce what is called a "Hawthorne effect" (people's reaction to an experiment) which cannot be identified, much less measured, but can undermine the scientific integrity of a social experiment.*

Although issues having to do with the process of obtaining informed consent are impressive, I believe that the most serious ethical issues concerning the treatment of human subjects come *after* informed consent has been obtained. Again, we can benefit from looking at an example. Suppose we are testing a home health-care program for the elderly and we design a demonstration using random assignment. Assume that the service is an expensive one and that the key dependent variable of interest to the funders and the researchers is whether this service over the long run reduces the cost of institutionalization in a hospital or nursing home. An older person comes into a senior citizen center and finds that she is eligible for this new "Home-Help" program being administered as a demonstration project. She is urged to sign up but is told that she may or may not be one of the participants selected. She decides to apply and fills out the necessary papers, which include several application and certification forms and also an informed consent agreement. Later, the program director checks by phone with the central research staff and discovers that this particular participant is assigned to the control group. The director is now face to face with the applicant and must tell her that she was

*The Hawthorne, or guinea pig, effect occurs when behavior is altered because people know they are being observed. Its name derives from studies at the Hawthorne Works of the Western Electric Company during the 1920s and 1930s. The studies showed continued productivity increases when lights were darkened and rest periods shortened, which researchers attributed to the additional attention paid to workers who knew they were part of an experiment. See Theodore H. Poister, *Public Program Analysis: Applied Research Methods* (Baltimore: University Park Press, 1970), pp. 266–67.

not selected for the program. The applicant asks, "Is there another program I can get into?" This raises a troublesome, yet not unusual, issue. Under these conditions, the program director knows that if the applicant is referred to another program, this may reduce the likelihood that the program that is the subject of this demonstration will have an impact. Yet that was usually the reason (to demonstrate such an impact) that the program director agreed to join the research project. We can call this the "program director's dilemma." The director in this case is between a rock and a hard place.

We can make this dilemma even more difficult if we assume that the program director is sitting across from an applicant who does *not* ask about another program, and the director knows about one that has openings. Should she make a referral even though it is unsolicited? There are no easy answers to these dilemmas.

Precisely because of these kinds of questions, the state of California undertook a large demonstration of a program similar to our hypothetical "Home-Help" program but did not use random assignment and did not even have a matched comparison group. The researchers used a mathematical model to estimate the experience of the target group without the program.[11] They compared the experience of the people in the demonstration program in terms of spells of institutionalization with norms for spells of institutionalization that had been established as benchmarks for comparison.

The results of this California study produced two problems. One was a familiar one. The impacts discerned were small, or at least they were so regarded by policymakers. The other problem, especially pertinent for our consideration of the treatment of human subjects, was that many observers (including key policymakers and other researchers) were skeptical and uncertain about what was inside the "black box," the assumptions and mathematical equations used to assess the program.

The tradeoff was between simplifying the research task, by virtue of not having to study nonparticipants, and the value to society of clear and credible findings in a demonstration study. In my view, the question that should be raised is not whether all studies that use simulation techniques, in part as a means of avoiding the research hurdles involved in treating human subjects, are a bad idea. Rather it is whether the way the relevant tradeoffs and decisions, as made in the California case or in any other case, are wise and well advised.

Uncertainty of Cost-Benefit Analysis

The eighth hurdle of demonstration research concerns cost-benefit analysis, which is often the last step in a demonstration research project. The usual procedure in demonstration research, with or without random assignment, is first to measure the short-term impact of a tested program on the participants. Then, as the final step in the research process, information about the cost of the program and the findings about its impact are integrated into a cost-benefit analysis, which seeks to identify the long-term *net* effect of the program being tested. Researchers often present their cost-benefit findings according to three perspectives—the net cost to the participants, to taxpayers (that is, to nonparticipants), and to society as a whole.

The aim of cost-benefit analysis is appealing. In an ideal world, one would want the rational policymaker to be in a position to compare the results of cost-benefit analyses for a range of program alternatives to achieve a particular policy objective and then to select the most effective one. This was the basic aim of Lyndon Johnson's planning-programming-budgeting system described in chapter 2, or at least it was the principal objective to which the PPB system aspired. But, as we know, the task of conducting demonstration research is so complicated, time-consuming, and expensive that we can only study a few programs in which we decide that the circumstances warrant the conduct of demonstration research. This means that no matter how good our intentions may be to use social science in making social policy, we will never be able to make policy "scientifically" on the basis of a wide range of cost-benefit findings for comparable programs.

Where demonstration studies are carried out, an obvious major purpose is to determine whether the tested program has had a sufficiently strong impact in the period in which it was studied to justify its replication on a broad basis. But this is not enough for some researchers and policymakers. They want to be able to assess the long-term net effect of the program. This involves substantial timing and data problems. Often, we do not have enough data for the out years, that is, projected forward beyond the study period. Moreover, attempts to ascertain the net cost-benefit ratio of a tested program sometimes encompass such a broad definition of program benefits that they go beyond the observed variables in a demonstration project by making assumptions or using proxies that are not understood by the users of cost-benefit analyses.

In my view, it is best to be *very cautious* about the use of cost-benefit analysis in demonstration research. Cost-benefit analysis is an uncertain art; I believe that it often detracts from the value of demonstration research and that as a general rule we are well advised to stop at the point of ascertaining the observed impacts of the tested program and let the political process take it from there.[12]

To summarize, my reasons for these conclusions are twofold: (1) there are likely to be unmeasured costs and benefits of a social demonstration that are left out of the cost-benefit equation or are such rough approximations as to be of questionable value; and (2) the methods for estimating the effects of a tested program beyond the study period are often highly uncertain. On the first point, the problem is that the variables (particularly the dependent variables) that are omitted from a demonstration study are often left out because they are difficult to quantify, perhaps even impossible to quantify. For example, in the case of the "Home-Help" for the elderly used earlier in this chapter, we may decide that the fact that the participants are happier in their own homes is a very important benefit. Yet, how would we monetize and measure this variable, which by implication some readers of research results are likely to think is part of our cost-benefit analysis?

A similar point can be made in the case of supported work. Policymakers may be interested in the effect of supported work on a distressed community or neighborhood. They may believe that in the long run a positive community effect is desirable for the society in and of itself and they may also believe that over time it will result in lower welfare costs. However, we would be hard put to measure these community effects in a demonstration study. The same holds for the effects of the supported-work program on children in welfare families. These dependent variables (effects on communities or children) were not included in the MDRC supported-work demonstration. However, the idea of a comprehensive cost-benefit analysis that purports to show the whole picture may suggest to some readers of the research results that these factors are part of what was studied.

Other types of benefits are often included in a cost-benefit analysis that are not well or easily measured. For example, in the case of the cost-benefit study of the Job Corps program, researchers found a cost-benefit ratio for the society of 1:1.46. This was regarded as a very good result. It needs to be noted, however, that 40 percent of the benefits came from reductions in criminal behavior, despite the obvious difficulty in measuring the costs to the society of crimes not committed. In the Job Corps case, the values assigned to injury and loss of life due to reduced criminal behavior had a very large effect on the cost-benefit findings. A murder was estimated to cost society $125,305.[13] The cost-benefit ratio of the Job Corps would have been negative—.8:1—if crime-reduction had not been considered and if increased production had been the only benefit considered.[14]

Rather than continuing down the cost-benefit road, I believe that social scientists who conduct demonstration studies should pull back in the interest of political realism and "truth in research." Furthermore, I believe as a general rule that instead of pushing for greater rigor in demonstration research, researchers should go in the opposite direction and broaden their net to study *more variables* on a less rigorous and more candid basis. Such an approach opts for breadth rather than depth of analysis and for short-term rather than longer-term impacts. This conclusion reflects the missing-links themes highlighted in the first chapter about the importance of blending different social science disciplines and also combining quantitative and qualitative data and methods in demonstration research.

The temporal dimension of the conventional practices of social science researchers in cost-benefit studies strengthens my argument for a less rigorous and more candid approach to this aspect of demonstration research. It was pointed out that the follow-up data in a demonstration study often do not cover as long a time period as is desired for the cost-benefit analysis. Under these conditions, researchers make assumptions about what are known as the "decay rates" of benefits over time. The literature on this subject is complex, but the key point is that decay rates are extremely difficult to measure. This is another "soft" ingredient that goes into the "black box" of cost-benefit analyses. In short, the task of assigning a specific number to net benefits in the out years of the programs tested in demonstration studies often gets researchers into a quagmire.

This is not to say that costs should be ignored in decisions about new programs, only that public policy researchers should focus their attention and analysis in demonstration research on *measured impacts*. They should tell policymakers what they measured, how they did it, and what they found. This knowledge should be combined by policy researchers and policy analysts with a number of other types of information, including the urgency of the problem, what is known about the impact (or lack of impact) of alternative approaches, and information about the costs of the tested program and of alternative programs.

Some readers may acknowledge the validity of the arguments made here but take the position that politicians want (even demand) one number—a clear, simple bottom-line result. This is often true. Still, I would argue that the scientific considerations outweigh these political arguments. Modesty and candor are required on the part of social science researchers in their dialogues with politicians about the uses and strengths and weaknesses of the findings from demonstration research.

Since I rely so heavily on the research conducted by MDRC, I am obliged to discuss MDRC's practice in the use of cost-benefit analysis. In most of its studies, MDRC has presented cost-benefit findings, but not without considerable soul-searching. When the board of the corporation issued its summary report on the national supported-work demonstration (the first demonstration research project conducted by MDRC), a carefully crafted statement about the limitations of cost-benefit analysis was included:

> Although the approach is useful in providing an overall assessment of supported work's effectiveness, it has limitations and risks. Certain important benefits and costs simply cannot be accurately measured and are therefore not included in the summary estimates. Moreover, this type of analysis calls for assumptions about

the value of specific items and for judgments on the longer term extrapolation of benefits and costs that were directly measured only for up to 27 or 36 months.[15]

Perhaps we should have stopped there. Labor economist Lloyd Ullman argues that the uncertainty of cost-benefit analysis produces an "expert witness" mentality whereby the proponents and opponents of a given program can trot out experts to argue both sides on a basis that often undermines the value of a well-conducted demonstration study.[16] At the very least, researchers should express cost-benefit findings in careful ways, using ranges of rounded numbers for their findings, and devising and presenting table formats that clearly and prominently indicate the major qualifications of this type of analysis.

For me, the hurdles to demonstration research considered in this chapter all point to the same conclusion: rigorous research on what works can be a useful and important input to the policy process despite the fact that it is not easy to do. After twenty years of experience with demonstration studies, we could not put this genie back into the bottle even if we wanted to. Politicians are bound to ask, Does it work? The capacity of social scientists to design and conduct demonstration research projects has increased but should be kept in perspective. Even under the best of circumstances, such studies are just *one of a number of inputs* to the policy process. Demonstration research is a useful tool for learning, consensus building, and education, but only under carefully defined conditions. As noted earlier, such studies are most effective when politicians care about a particular issue, are genuinely uncertain about how to handle it, and are willing to wait for the findings of a research project. I have found that many politicians are interested in studies of what works. A great deal of goodwill, common purpose, and serious interest in the potential of demonstration research in the domestic policy process exists on the part of many government officials.

Despite this conclusion that we are on a rising learning curve for demonstration research, and that there is considerable demand for such studies, we still have a tendency to look for a single bottom-line answer and to attempt (as in the case of cost-benefit analysis) to achieve greater rigor and precision than the artform can support.

The effective conduct of demonstration studies can produce in-depth expertise on the part of the participating scholars about both the inputs and the outputs of government action. This is a valuable resource for public policymaking. Demonstration studies also can be valuable to social science scholarship. The experience of the Manpower Demonstration Research Corporation discussed in the next chapter shows how policy and scientific knowledge can be developed and used in a manner that benefits both social policy and social science.

5

Studies by the
Manpower Demonstration
Research Corporation

THIS CHAPTER uses studies conducted by the Manpower Demonstration Research Corporation to illustrate how demonstration research ties into the policy process. The Manpower Demonstration Research Corporation is a nonprofit intermediary corporation based in New York City that manages demonstration research projects using funds from governments (federal, state, and local) and foundations. The studies undertaken by MDRC have focused on the most disadvantaged groups in society; the studies emphasize job training, employment, and related social service programs. By 1987, MDRC had conducted or was planning eight large-scale demonstration studies plus a number of smaller projects.

The MDRC came into existence in 1974 to conduct the national supported-work demonstration. The role and form of the corporation is a function of the decisions made about the conduct of this original demonstration. The supported-work program was developed by the Vera Institute of Justice of New

York City as a way to provide employment for people accused of minor offenses in the criminal justice system. The aim was to provide participants with work experience in a group situation under conditions of gradually increasing stress. An operating subsidiary of the Vera Institute, the Wildcat Service Corporation, was established in 1969 to run the supported-work program; its roster grew from 6 participants in the fall of 1969 to nearly 1,400 in mid-1974. Participants worked in jobs such as cleaning, plastering, and painting buildings being restored; clearing refuse from vacant lots; serving as messengers; providing building- and park-maintenance services; clearing construction sites; interpreting for Spanish-speaking hospital patients; and driving for the elderly.

Early studies of the Vera-Wildcat supported-work program showed promising results.[1] As a consequence, Mitchell Sviridoff, then vice-president for national affairs of the Ford Foundation, decided to explore the feasibility of a national study of the supported-work idea. Sviridoff sought assistance from a number of federal agencies and established a research committee on which I served to advise the Ford Foundation in this area. The advisory committee, headed by Eli Ginzberg of Columbia University, recommended a multisite national demonstration with participants randomly assigned to either a supported-work program or a control group. Six federal agencies, with the Department of Labor as the lead agency, committed funds to this research, which began in March 1975. Over the full three-year period of the supported-work demonstration, 10,000 people were assigned as participants. A total of 6,616 people were in the research sample, 3,214 as participants and 3,402 in the control group.

As the planning for this national demonstration moved into high gear, it became apparent that the managerial task was a formidable one. The list of participating organizations was growing—the Ford Foundation, six federal agencies, the fifteen sites operating the program (ten of them research sites), the research contractors, plus a central staff to coordinate and manage the demonstration. By mid-1974, the total cost of the demonstration, including funds from local sources, was estimated at $80 million, most of which was ultimately spent on the participants in the tested programs.

The assumption up until this time had been that an interagency committee of federal government officials would manage the supported-work demonstration. However, as the planning process proceeded, it became increasingly clear that an interagency coordinating committee would have great difficulty handling the ongoing management tasks for such a complicated and dispersed research project. It was decided in May 1974 to convert the research advisory committee for the study into a nonprofit corporation, chartered in Delaware, which would receive funds from a consortium of federal agencies and the Ford Foundation to manage the demonstration. Because this intermediary corporation formed for the demonstration proved to be an effective management device, it has continued in existence to conduct other demonstration research projects for disadvantaged groups. The original members of the corporate board (all academic social scientists) were Eli Ginzberg, Robert Lampman, Richard Nathan, Robert Solow, Gilbert Steiner, and Phyllis Wallace. Ginzberg chaired the board from 1974 to 1981 when he was succeeded by the author. The first president of the corporation was William G. Grinker; he was succeeded in July 1982 by Barbara Blum. Blum served until September 1986 when she was succeeded by Judith M. Gueron, who has been an officer of the corporation since its inception, heading MDRC's research staff.

In addition to the supported-work demonstration, seven major demonstration studies have been conducted by MDRC: (1) a study of the tenant management approach to administer public housing projects; (2) a saturation guaranteed-job program known as the Youth Incentive Entitlement Pilot Project, which was established by federal law as a demonstration project; (3) Project Redirection to provide services to very young women receiving welfare benefits; (4) an employment and training program (called the WIN Laboratory Project*) conducted in Louisville, Kentucky; (5) the Structured Training and Employment Transition Services demonstration (a program similar to supported work) for young mentally retarded workers; (6) an eight-state test of work/welfare approaches to welfare reform; and (7) an intensive remediation and training program for school dropouts called Jobstart. An additional demonstration was initiated in 1988, New Chance, a comprehensive service program for very young welfare mothers.

As the Manpower Demonstration Research Corporation gained experience, it moved from relatively small and focused pilot projects to evaluation research on larger ongoing programs. The best example of the latter is the corporation's evaluation of the statewide work/welfare program in California. The discussion of the MDRC experience in this chapter highlights the corporation's early demonstration research. In chapter 6 and the following chapters, the discussion shifts to MDRC's newer evaluation research activities. I begin with MDRC's first study, the national supported-work demonstration; my purpose here is to take a close look at the linkages between social science research and social policy in the field of public welfare.

---

*WIN is the acronym used for the Work Incentive Program, a federal grant-in-aid program to the states to provide employment and training services to welfare family heads.

Supported Work and Welfare Reform

Since the early 1970s welfare reform for able-bodied individuals of working age and their families has been the Mount Everest of U.S. domestic policy. There are two basic approaches to welfare reform. One is the *income strategy*, which underlies the negative income tax idea. The basic aim of this approach is to change the structure of welfare benefits in order to provide an incentive for working-age, able-bodied poor people to enter and stay in the labor force. The other major approach to welfare reform is the *service strategy*, which emphasizes such services as counseling and job placement, training, remedial and vocational education, and child care to help move people from the welfare rolls and enable them to enter the regular work force.

In 1962 under President Kennedy the federal government enacted legislation to provide counseling, job training, and related rehabilitative services to able-bodied welfare family heads, reflecting the service approach to welfare reform. Later, toward the end of the 1960s, the emphasis of national welfare policy shifted to the income strategy. The negative income tax demonstrations were initiated in 1968, and in 1969 President Nixon proposed his Family Assistance Plan for welfare reform. Although Nixon's proposal was a hybrid of the income and service approaches, the newest and most widely discussed features of his plan were those that involved the negative income tax approach to welfare reform.

The supported-work demonstration, even though it was not initiated with this as its main purpose, reflected the service approach to welfare reform. The demonstration began in 1974 not long after the last rites were administered for Nixon's Family Assistance Plan. The idea of supported work is that disadvantaged people of working age should be "supported" as they enter the work force; as they become increasingly better adjusted to the workplace this support is gradually withdrawn. The aim is to help participants acquire work skills that enable them to become regular members of the labor force. The experiences of working with peers, meeting deadlines, and relating to supervisors are seen as skills that can help disadvantaged people move into and stay in unsupported jobs.

The supported-work program, as originally developed by the Vera Institute of Justice, did not apply to welfare family heads. It focused on criminal–justice system offenders as an alternative to incarceration. The aim of MDRC's national demonstration was to test this approach on a broader basis, both geographically and in terms of the groups included. Which groups should be the target populations for the national demonstration? A key factor was money. The funders of the demonstration, particularly the federal agencies involved, had different interests and constituencies. The Labor Department was interested in youth. The Department of Justice was interested in previous offenders. The drug-abuse prevention agency was interested in former addicts.

The Department of Health, Education, and Welfare initially was reluctant to participate in the funding consortium for the national supported-work demonstration. Caspar Weinberger, at that time secretary of HEW, apparently had reservations about the administrative arrangement involving a nonprofit intermediary corporation to coordinate and manage demonstration research. Although HEW eventually provided funds for the supported-work demonstration, a decision was made by MDRC prior to HEW's decision to participate to include long-term welfare family heads as one of the major target groups in the demonstration. This was done on the assumption that MDRC could use Ford Foundation and some federal funds to serve this group. As it turned out, this was a fortuitous decision. Altogether there were four target groups in

TABLE 5.1

Supported-Work Eligibility Criteria, by Target Group

Target Group	Eligibility Criteria[a]
AFDC	Women on AFDC both currently and for 30 out of the preceding 36 months; youngest child 6 years old or older
Ex-addicts	Age 18 years or older; enrolled in a drug treatment program currently or within the preceding 6 months
Ex-offenders	Age 18 years or older; incarcerated within the last 6 months as a result of a conviction
Youths	Age 17 to 20 years; no high school or equivalency degree; not in school in the last 6 months; delinquency record, conviction, court appearance, or similar (for at least 50% of the youth)
All groups	Currently unemployed[b]; spent no more than 3 months in a job during the past 6 months

Source: Board of Directors, Manpower Demonstration Research Corporation, *Summary and Findings of the National Supported Work Demonstration* (Cambridge, Mass.: Ballinger, 1980), p. 23.
[a]Supported work eligibility criteria refer to conditions prevailing at the time of application to the supported-work program. If a person in supported work voluntarily or involuntarily leaves the program and subsequently reapplies for a supported-work job, he or she is not reviewed again for acceptance under the eligibility criteria.
[b]Worked no more than 10 hours a week for the last 4 weeks.

the supported-work demonstration—problem youth, former offenders (that is, persons who had previously been incarcerated as a result of a conviction for a criminal offense), former narcotic addicts, and long-term female welfare family heads (see table 5.1).

The definition of target groups was only the beginning. Many other decisions had to be made. Since this was the first demonstration project conducted by MDRC, the learning process was more difficult and time-consuming than for the later demonstrations conducted by the corporation.

Conduct of the Supported-Work Demonstration

As the supported-work demonstration got under way, discussions within the corporation came to reflect an increasingly more sophisticated view of the challenges to be faced. Eli Ginzberg, chairman of the board of MDRC, and a master at getting to the heart of issues, produced the following notes from one of the early meetings in this planning process:

- The best-designed and controlled social experiment can never take account of exogenous factors.
- The odds are very strong that any social intervention will be too weak to show clear-cut positive effects.
- Many types of effects cannot be caught in even the most sophisticated evaluation.
- Because of hidden bias in clients and selectors, the matching of experimentals and controls is likely to be flawed.

As suggested by Ginzberg's notes, all of the research hurdles discussed in the previous chapter were confronted in the planning and execution of this research. At the outset, concern about selection bias and the null hypothesis led to a decision to test what was regarded as a relatively long (nine months to one year) treatment compared to the experience of a randomly assigned control group. The decision to adopt random assignment was an integral part of the research design for this study from the outset.

Despite the fact that HEW funds were not initially included in the demonstration, the corporation decided to set up its own human subjects review board headed by MDRC board member Gilbert Y. Steiner. (None of the review board members except Steiner were members of the MDRC board.) In turn, the MDRC review board decided to adopt the HEW rules for the treatment of human subjects in demonstration research.

This meant that an "informed-consent" agreement would be obtained from all participants in the supported-work demonstration. In the design process for the demonstration, both the review board and the corporation board wrestled with the ethical issues involved in not providing services to people in the control group. This was justified on the grounds that since the service to be provided was necessarily limited in its coverage, allocating it on a random basis was fair.

The fifteen sponsoring organizations of supported-work projects at the local level typically were small nonprofit organizations. Of course, the possibility existed that the project would have what was described in chapter 4 as "service contamination." However, the fact that most other available employment and training programs for the eligible population in the communities studied were much shorter in duration and less intensive was seen as a likely factor that would mitigate against this problem.

At the outset of the research process, considerable staff and board time were devoted to the selection of research contractors. Later, the relationship with these contractors was the focus of a major controversy over prospective cost overruns that resulted in protracted bargaining sessions to prevent this from happening. Robert Solow (then vice-chairman of the MDRC board) and I (then treasurer) participated in extensive, detailed negotiations with the main research contractor, Mathematica Policy Research of Princeton, New Jersey. (Mathematica had a similar leading role in the New Jersey negative income tax demonstrations.) Mathematica researchers conducted the baseline and follow-up surveys of supported-work participants and controls and were responsible for the impact and cost-benefit studies with help from researchers at the Institute for Research on Poverty at the University of Wisconsin.

Results of the Demonstration

The most important findings of the national supported-work demonstration involved the differences in impact among the four treatment groups. The impact of supported work was largest for the AFDC group. The summary report on this demonstration stated, "The program has proved most effective in preparing for employment a substantial number of women who have been on welfare (AFDC) for many years."[2] Table 5.2 shows the results by time period for the AFDC group. The most important period is the nineteen to twenty-seven month postenrollment period. The difference between the experimental participants and the controls in the earlier periods (one to eighteen months) in hours worked and earnings were likely to have been a result of the fact that the welfare family heads in the treatment groups were enrolled in the supported-work program during this period.

The 8.5 percent difference in the percentage employed between the demonstration group and the controls in the period nineteen to twenty-seven months after enrollment is statistically significant at the 5 percent level. The treatment group worked nearly sixteen hours more per month than the controls and earned an average of $77 per month more than the controls. Their welfare and food stamp benefits were reduced by an average of 14 percent for AFDC and a like proportion for food stamps. In short, supported work was successful for the AFDC group, although the gains made were not large or dramatic.

For the former addict group (see table 5.3) the results were also positive, but less strong.

A close reader of these two tables will notice an important point. The impact of the supported-work program for the AFDC group is in large part a result of the fact that the

TABLE 5.2

Experimental-Control Differences during 27 Months Following Enrollment, AFDC Group

Outcome Measure	Experimentals	Controls	Difference
Percent employed during period			
Months 1–9	96.3	36.5	59.8[c]
10–18	76.5	39.4	37.1[c]
19–27	49.1	40.6	8.5[c]
Average monthly hours worked			
Months 1–9	135.3	26.6	108.7[c]
10–18	79.4	40.3	39.1[c]
19–27	60.9	45.2	15.7[c]
Average monthly earnings ($)			
Months 1–9	400.44	78.28	322.16[c]
10–18	274.06	131.08	142.98[c]
19–27	242.89	165.88	77.01[c]
Cash welfare payments[a]			
(Percent receiving)			
Months 1–9	93.8	97.7	−3.9[c]
10–18	82.4	90.1	−7.7[c]
19–27	71.4	85.1	−13.7[c]
Average monthly amount ($)			
Months 1–9	169.82	277.90	−108.09[c]
10–18	164.28	246.60	−82.32[c]
19–27	172.06	224.00	−51.94[c]
Food stamps: average monthly bonus value ($)			
Months 1–9	44.83	63.46	−18.63[c]
10–18	42.15	58.02	−15.87[c]
19–27	47.14	60.25	−13.11[c]
Average monthly total income ($)[b]			
Months 1–9	628.06	435.10	192.96[c]
10–18	524.47	454.44	70.03[c]
19–27	497.50	470.14	27.36

Source: Board of Directors, Manpower Demonstration Research Corporation, *Summary and Findings of the National Supported Work Demonstration* (Cambridge, Mass.: Ballinger, 1980), p. 153.
Note: Averages are calculated for all members of the sample, including those with no employment or transfer payment receipt in the covered period.
[a]Welfare includes AFDC, General Assistance, Supplemental Security Income, and other unspecified cash welfare.
[b]Total income includes earnings, unemployment compensation, welfare, food stamp bonus value, and other unearned income (Social Security, pensions, alimony, and child support).
[c]Statistically significant at the 5 percent level.

TABLE 5.3

*Experimental-Control Differences during 36 Months
Following Enrollment, Ex-Addict Group*

Outcome Measure		Experimentals	Controls	Difference
Percent employed during period				
Months	1–9	95.0	50.2	44.8[b]
	10–18	63.9	53.1	10.8[b]
	19–27	56.5	53.0	3.5
	28–36	64.0	53.9	10.1[c]
Average monthly hours worked				
Months	1–9	118.7	40.5	78.2[b]
	10–18	66.4	50.0	16.4[b]
	19–27	60.1	58.6	1.5
	28–36	70.9	52.6	18.3[b]
Average monthly earnings ($)				
Months	1–9	361.23	159.79	201.44[b]
	10–18	259.62	220.42	39.20[c]
	19–27	277.75	261.33	16.42
	28–36	326.09	224.36	101.73[b]
Average monthly welfare and food stamps benefits ($)[a]				
Months	1–9	57.97	115.17	−57.20[b]
	10–18	92.42	110.89	−18.47[b]
	19–27	89.90	93.94	−4.04
	28–36	94.34	103.79	−9.45
Percent using any drug other than marijuana or alcohol				
Months	1–9	36.1	38.2	−2.1
	10–18	34.1	32.7	1.4
	19–27	28.0	27.5	0.5
	28–36	23.4	20.7	2.7
Percent using heroin				
Months	1–9	20.2	21.5	−1.3
	10–18	16.8	17.8	−1.0
	19–27	13.4	11.7	1.7
	28–36	10.1	8.8	1.3
Percent arrested				
Months	1–18	25.3	33.5	−8.2[b]
	1–36	35.0	53.1	−18.1[b]
Percent arrested for robbery				
Months	1–18	2.3	7.5	−5.2[b]
	1–36	0.2	13.4	−13.2[b]

TABLE 5.3 *(Continued)*

Outcome Measure	Experimentals	Controls	Difference
Percent arrested on drug			
charges			
Months 1–18	4.1	7.9	−3.8[b]
1–36	6.8	14.0	−7.2
Percent convicted			
Months 1–18	13.5	17.8	−4.3[c]
1–36	19.3	32.9	−13.6[c]

Source: Board of Directors, Manpower Demonstration Research Corporation, *Summary and Findings of the National Supported Work Demonstration* (Cambridge, Mass.: Ballinger, 1980), p. 155.
Note: Averages are calculated for all members of the sample, including those with no employment or transfer payment receipt in the covered period.
[a]Welfare includes AFDC, General Assistance, Supplemental Security Income, and other unspecified cash welfare.
[b]Statistically significant at the 5 percent level.
[c]Statistically significant at the 10 percent level.

controls fared relatively poorly in the labor market. (Compare, for example, the labor market experience of the AFDC and former addicts control groups in tables 5.2 and 5.3.) Similar findings have been made in other studies. The problems of AFDC family heads are so serious in terms of their ability to enter and participate in the labor market that an intervention with this group is likely to have a bigger impact than for other groups. Society, in effect, gains more from "investing" in programs for this group.

The significance of this finding has to do with what is known as "creaming" in job training and work experience programs. Both the managers of training programs and employers often see themselves as benefiting from a focus on the most job-ready people in the eligible population. They are the ones most likely to "make it" in the labor market, providing employers with reliable workers and putting the program sponsors in a position to claim success for their efforts. But the point is often missed that the most job-ready participants are likely to make it anyway; the tested program is not providing value added under these circumstances. Targeting, as in the case of the long-term female welfare family heads in the supported-work demonstration, is more likely to produce a positive program impact.

For the other two groups in the demonstration—problem youth and previous offenders—the results showed no or very little impact of the supported work. According to the summary report on the national demonstration, the program did not yield long-term positive results for the youth group. It had a marginal impact on former offenders.

Implications for Welfare Reform

The supported-work demonstration was initiated in 1974 during a period in which generally liberal attitudes on social policy issues predominated. But by the time MDRC had finished the demonstration and published and disseminated the results, it was 1980. The tide had turned. Supported work had been successful for welfare family heads, but unfortunately it was seen by many politicians and public officials in 1980 as too expensive to be replicated on a broad basis.

This initial reaction to the findings of the supported-work demonstration for welfare family heads proved to be short-lived. As the results became more widely known, government officials at every level (national, state, and local) began to notice the central finding about the employability of AFDC recipients and sought to replicate supported work or derivative concepts. In 1981 and following, as President Reagan's plans for welfare were developed and advanced, the lessons of the supported-work demonstration came to play an important role in his efforts to scale this Everest of domestic policy. Reagan's policies in this field are the subject of this section.

In his second term as governor of California, Ronald Reagan

made welfare reform a central issue of his administration. Experts debate the degree to which Reagan's efforts succeeded, but for Reagan there were no doubts: "When I took office, California was the welfare capital of the nation. The caseload was increasing 40,000 a month. We turned that 40,000 a month increase into an 8,000 a month decrease. We returned to the taxpayers $2 billion and we increased grants to the truly needy by forty-three percent." According to Fred C. Doolittle, the California Welfare Reform Act passed in 1971 "marked a turning point in the political career of Ronald Reagan."[3]

Reagan's biographer Lou Cannon similarly views the welfare reform battle as "Reagan's transformation from communicator to governor."[4] Reagan's initial involvement in welfare reform coincided with the decidedly more liberal welfare reform efforts of the Nixon administration at the national level beginning in 1969. In fact, from the Nixon period forward, liberal and conservative reform strategies vied with each other in the welfare field. Through much of the 1970s, the result was a stalemate. Reagan was a leading proponent of the conservative position. His advocacy of state government authority over welfare met strong resistance from liberals. Meanwhile, Nixon's and Carter's more centralized proposals to replace the AFDC program with a comprehensive new payment system with features of a negative income tax were stymied, although some important liberalizing changes were made in other welfare program areas.[5]

In the case of the AFDC program, however, basic change was resisted. Responsibility for the AFDC program continues to be shared among the federal government and the states and, in some cases, counties. Payment levels and eligibility criteria for AFDC vary from state to state. Disparities in grant levels among the states are substantial; benefits in 1987 ranged from $749 per month for a family of three in Alaska and $617 in California to $118 in Alabama and $120 in Mississippi.[6]

As governor of California, Ronald Reagan, along with other

conservatives, opposed centralizing and liberalizing efforts to overhaul the AFDC program as embodied in the Nixon FAP. Despite the fact that they are both Republicans, Nixon and Reagan have had a history of difficult and sometimes frosty relations. Reagan not only was a leader among conservatives in opposing Nixon's welfare reform plans, he offered his own counterproposals. In testimony before the Senate Finance Committee in 1972, Reagan presented his state-based California approach to welfare reform as a model for national legislation. He boasted that these proposals "are the product of our experience with an *actual* reform program that is succeeding in California, they are not a theory."[7] Reagan's California program consisted of increased benefits for the "truly needy," reduced benefits or no benefits for the "working poor," and "workfare," which Reagan defined as the mandatory-work approach. Rather than centralizing the AFDC program, Reagan favored turning it over to the states in the form of a block grant under which the states would receive a lump-sum amount to use on a flexible basis to aid poor families.

There is a paradox in Reagan's role in the debate on welfare policy. Despite his consistent and strong support for the decentralization approach to welfare, Reagan was much more successful at the national level as president than he was at the state level as governor of California in advancing his conservative welfare reform ideas. Considerable controversy exists over whether Reagan's California reforms reduced welfare costs and caseloads; his "workfare" plan resulted in minuscule participation by welfare recipients in mandatory public service jobs. On the other hand, Reagan's biggest gains in terms of advancing his welfare policy goals came at the national level. In the 1981 federal budget act, Reagan managed to win approval for AFDC policy changes that had the effect of tightening national eligibility and benefit rules under AFDC in a way that reduced the number of working family heads on the AFDC and Medicaid rolls and cut benefits for many other families.[8]

The 1981 budget act as a whole was Reagan's most important and successful challenge to the domestic programs of the
federal government. His 1981 changes to scale back the work-
incentive features of the AFDC program (provisions that had
been added in 1967) had the effect of reducing the AFDC rolls
by about 10 percent and cutting benefits for the people who
remained by a like proportion. Research on the effects of these
changes indicated that they did not result in an increase in
applicants and recipients as some had predicted would be the
effect of reducing the work-incentive features of AFDC.[9]

For purposes of this discussion of the role of social science
research in public policymaking, the most important element
of the Reagan welfare reform strategy is "workfare." The word
itself has an interesting history. It was first used on a general
basis in Nixon's television address to the nation on 8 August
1969, on his New Federalism domestic program. "What
America needs now," said Nixon, "is not more welfare, but
more 'workfare.' "[10] Nixon intended that his welfare reform
plan should be known by this term. But the word *workfare* in
general usage came to have a much narrower and harsher
meaning, referring only to mandatory work for welfare family
heads. I have never been able to pin down why the term came
to have this conservative work-for-your-welfare meaning. The
best explanation I have found is that the press attached this
term to alternatives to Nixon's FAP proposed by Senator Russell Long (D-La.), then chairman of the Senate Finance Committee. Long's approach limited assistance payments to em-
ployable needy family heads to compensation for work
performed. In any event, the term *workfare* became an anath-
ema to liberals in the 1970s, often lambasted by them as
"slavefare."

In his 1971 California welfare reform program, Reagan advocated workfare as a reflection of this narrower mandatory
work concept. A decade later as president, Reagan again made
workfare a key component of his welfare reform strategy,

proposing in 1981 that workfare (again using this narrower definition) be made compulsory and nationwide. However, Congress was reluctant to go along with this part of Reagan's 1981 welfare reform plan. Although the Congress accepted most of Reagan's recommended welfare changes (of AFDC rules regarding benefit levels and eligibility as mentioned earlier), it would only agree to give the states authority to implement the workfare approach on a trial basis.

One might have thought that this would be the end of workfare. Yet, even though it was relegated to a pilot program, it did get off the ground (although gradually) as an element of Reagan's presidential welfare policy. Ironically, however, under President Reagan the meaning of workfare changed in subtle ways despite the conservative mood of the country in the 1980s. The workfare idea was broadened; it became "new-style workfare" in the hands of state governments.

New-style workfare involves a range of services, including remedial and vocational education, job training and counseling, and community work experience. By 1987 over half the states had adopted such a multiservice strategy in an effort to convert their welfare payment systems into systems focused on job preparation, work, and the reduction of welfare dependency. Many of these state initiatives were launched under the banner of Reagan's 1981 welfare policy changes. In the usual way in American federalism, these new state programs vary according to the different values, aims, and economic conditions of state governments. Although "new-style workfare" as interpreted by states continues to be opposed by some liberals, criticism of this broader concept has diminished since 1981. Increasingly, welfare advocates and program administrators have come to accept this employment and training approach to welfare reform as a means to enhance the public image of welfare as a work-oriented system. Many state officials, especially the administrators of social programs, appear to have adopted this strategy as a means ultimately to improve the image of welfare and increase the willingness of voters to provide more generous levels of assistance to welfare families. The politics of this shift of opinion on the part of welfare professionals are interesting. It is not clear who is coopting whom. Are the conservatives winning the day, or are liberals using the workfare idea as an instrument for converting the welfare system into job-focused service systems more acceptable to the public?

Up to now, I have referred to the workfare portion of the 1981 federal budget act in the singular. Actually, there were three employment and training provisions in this act allowing the states to test new work/welfare approaches. One provision is the Community Work Experience Program (CWEP). It authorizes the states to use AFDC funds to pay eligible family heads for public service work. There had been a different program called "CWEP" under Reagan when he was governor of California. In this earlier period, however, it was the *California* work experience program rather than the *community* work experience program. A second employment and training provision of the 1981 budget act sponsored by Senator Russell Long, then ranking minority member of the Senate Finance Committee, gives states the authority to provide subsidies for on-the-job training programs for AFDC recipients by diverting welfare grants to wage subsidies to private employers. (This authority is referred to as "grant diversion.") The chief distinction between grant diversion and CWEP is that grant diversion provides jobs for welfare recipients in the private sector, whereas CWEP operates in the public sector. The third 1981 work/welfare amendment authored by Senators Moynihan (D-N.Y.) and David Boren (D-Okla.) turned out to be much more important than observers had originally expected. Its purpose was to overhaul the Work Incentive Program (WIN), originally enacted in 1967 to provide funding and authority for the states to run job placement, training, and related service programs for AFDC family heads as a means of reducing welfare dependency. Up until 1981, state WIN programs were required to be jointly administered by the state employment service and welfare agency. Moynihan argued that this requirement for joint management, which he said often resulted in "byzantine administrative arrangements," should be changed to allow states to set up demonstration programs so the WIN program could be run by a single state agency on a much more flexible basis.

This history is significant for two reasons. One involves the policy connection between the supported-work demonstration and what is referred to here as "new-style workfare." The other, and for present purposes more important, connection between supported work and new-style workfare involves agenda setting for applied social science research.

It was in this policy environment of the implementation of the 1981 welfare changes that MDRC began in the following year to work with eight state governments to conduct a series of demonstration studies on the efforts by these states to apply one or several of the new work/welfare provisions in the 1981 budget act. For MDRC, these studies can be viewed as a "New Federalism" approach to public policy research. The MDRC used challenge-grant funds from the Ford Foundation to pay part of the costs of the research and the states (or in some cases foundations within the states) provided the remaining funds needed for the research. (Program funds for these demonstrations, as opposed to the research funds to conduct the demonstrations, were provided by the federal government on a matching basis.)

These MDRC work/welfare demonstrations are in effect tests of different ways in which the states have attempted to reform their welfare systems, often in a portion of the state rather than statewide, to strengthen their work orientation in ways that draw on the authority provided in the 1981 budget act. (The Virginia and West Virginia programs stand out as geographically broad-gauged; MDRC's studies, although not statewide, were extensive in these two cases.)

From a political point of view, the important characteristic of these work/welfare demonstrations is that the research agenda was part of a larger effort by politicians at the national level and in the states to reform welfare systems. The connection between social science and social policy in this case was very different from the case of the negative income tax experiments of a decade earlier where the research agenda was set by social scientists. It was different also from the earlier MDRC research projects in which politicians had much less of a role in influencing the research agenda.

Appropriately, in light of the fact that Ronald Reagan was a former governor of the state, the first state to enter the MDRC work/welfare demonstration was California. The demonstration in this case was conducted in San Diego County. Beginning in August 1982, San Diego County assigned more than 5,000 AFDC family heads to two programs adopted under the 1981 work/welfare amendments. Another 2,000 people were assigned randomly to a control group. Two programs were tested, a group job-search system (called a "job club") and a combination of a job club followed by assignment to community work experience in cases when participants in the job club did not find employment through these or related job-search efforts. The work experience component of the San Diego demonstration lasted thirteen weeks and was limited to thirty-two hours per week.[11]

Officials of San Diego County have had a long-standing interest in programs of this type. The county had undertaken similar employment and training projects related to the AFDC and food stamp programs. In the case of this particular AFDC work/welfare program, the state Employment Development

Department (California's employment service agency) contracted with MDRC to conduct the research for this demonstration. Seven other states also participated in the MDRC work/welfare demonstration: Arkansas, Illinois, Maine, Maryland, New Jersey, Virginia, and West Virginia. Altogether, 35,000 people participated on a random-assignment basis in this demonstration research.

Although both the nature and scope of these state demonstrations were varied, there are common elements. In all of the demonstration states, with the exception of New Jersey and Maine, where the demonstration was limited to private-sector grant diversion, there was some degree of *obligation*, that is, welfare family heads in the treatment group were required to *do something* in order to receive their benefits. "Doing something" could refer to job search, participation in a job club or a training or education program, a period of community work experience, acceptance of an available job, or some sequenced combination of these and other elements.

The basic approach did not represent a new idea for public policy. Repeated efforts have been made at both the national and state levels to require welfare family heads (usually those with children above preschool age) to search for employment, to accept a "suitable" job if one is offered, and in some cases also to participate in training programs. What is distinctive about these new state efforts is that this obligation was supposed to be taken *seriously*. Persons who did not cooperate were supposed to be sanctioned. One can think of these efforts as converting AFDC from an *entitlement* program into a *conditional* program.[12] Recipients were no longer automatically entitled to receive AFDC benefits; they were required to participate in these new-style state workfare programs as a condition of receiving AFDC benefits.

There was considerable variation among the eight states in the MDRC work/welfare demonstration in the character and degree of obligation of the tested programs. On the one hand, the San Diego project and the West Virginia project for males in the welfare caseload emphasized the mandatory nature of the program, whereas in Maryland this feature of the program was included but not as strongly emphasized. All of these demonstrations can be thought of as an attempt to use these demonstration research projects as *an agent of institutional change.* The basic aim is to change the welfare system in the direction of imposing employment-related requirements and facilitating movement into the labor force.

Among the main findings of the eight MDRC work/welfare demonstration studies are the following:

1. In most cases, the work/welfare projects had positive impacts, although the size of these impacts was generally modest.
2. These positive effects were a result both of increased earnings on the part of participants, mostly female welfare family heads, and reduced welfare benefits.
3. In some states, there was a deterrent effect (that is, deterring welfare recipients as suggested by a welfare reduction without demonstrable associated employment gains). On the whole, this deterrent effect tended to be stronger for males in two-parent AFDC households than for female welfare family heads in single-parent households. This is an important point for conservatives, because it suggests that some welfare recipients could not participate in work/welfare programs because they had unreported or underground employment.
4. Consistent with earlier findings, these demonstrations showed that females who head welfare families tended to register the largest gains, that is, compared to male parents in two-parent welfare families.
5. Participants with serious problems tended to register relatively larger gains than more experienced and better-qualified workers. Again, this finding is consistent with what has been learned from earlier studies. It constitutes an argument against "creaming" (favoring the most qualified participants) under employment and training programs.

6. The jobs provided were generally useful; they were not "make-work" jobs, although they were not skilled jobs either.
7. Participants in these programs who were surveyed about their attitude toward the program were generally positive in their ratings of the program. They tended to believe that the mandatory approach was fair. In fact, a problem noted in one jurisdiction was that people assigned to the control group complained that they were not allowed to participate in the mandatory services.[13]

An important point for this book is the connection between this demonstration research and the follow-up evaluation research in California. The connection is twofold, involving both the substance of policy and the conduct of policy research. State officials in California, in part on the basis of what they learned in the San Diego demonstration, decided that the employment approach to welfare reform should be adopted on a general basis in the state. In this case, the findings of a demonstration study are linked to the new statewide policy. This demonstration also had major implications for MDRC. It led to a new role for the corporation—specifically the conduct of an evaluation study of the statewide work/welfare program that has been adopted by California. Before proceeding to discuss evaluation studies, we do well to take an inventory on the lessons learned from the conduct of demonstration studies as discussed in chapters 3 through 5.

Lessons Learned

Considerable political and managerial skill is required to bring social scientists and politicians together so that demonstration research deals with problems politicians care about, under conditions in which they are interested in what works and are willing to wait to find out. This analysis stresses the desirability of giving substantial (and generally higher) priority in demonstration research to the institutional dimension of a tested policy change. We need to know what is in the "black box," how the treatment works, what agencies and organizations are involved, and how they operate. The analysis also emphasizes the missing links between social science disciplines and variables, and between quantitative and qualitative research methods in the design and conduct of these studies. I believe psychologists, sociologists, and political scientists should be given larger roles in demonstration studies.

In sum, we have learned that demonstration studies are difficult, expensive, and time-consuming. Hence the treatments to be tested must be carefully selected. We have also learned that random assignment is a strong tool. The hard problems of working out relationships with program operators, collecting adequate data, and protecting the interests of human subjects have been critical areas of the learning process of demonstration research. Although not everyone in the field would agree, in my view the experience to date raises questions about the wisdom of cost-benefit analysis as the final step in a demonstration study.

6

Evaluation Research

EUGENE BARDACH, in a book on what he calls "the implementation game," makes a point that is recurrent in the political science literature on American government: "It is hard enough to design public policies and programs that look good on paper." It is harder still to sell them to the public. "And it is excruciatingly hard to implement them in a way that pleases anyone at all, including the supposed beneficiaries and clients."[1] In a similar vein, Clinton Rossiter said that many U.S. presidents have found that their hardest job is "not to persuade Congress to support a policy dear to his political heart, but to persuade the pertinent bureau or agency—even when headed by men of his own choosing—to follow his direction faithfully and transform the shadow of the policy into the substance of the program."[2]

One does not have to be a close student of American government to know that there is often a great gap between setting policy objectives and carrying them out. According to Angela Browne and Aaron Wildavsky, "Policy implementation is hypothesis testing: It is *exploration.*"[3] An explorer cannot predict what will be discovered. Every voyage is different. Political scientists can tell us that program implementation is complex and unpredictable. But how do we use this insight to answer questions politicians may have about what happens once a new policy is adopted?

A major claim of this book is that there is both an opportunity and a need to develop better research approaches for evaluation research on the effects of policies once they have been adopted and the implementation process is under way. We need to look closely at how and why evaluation research differs from demonstration research. Three such reasons are featured in this chapter.

Limits in Control over Programs

Compared to a demonstration study, researchers have less control over the conditions under which an evaluation study is carried out. We have already seen that the ability of researchers to control the environment in a demonstration study is much more limited than might appear at first. But such problems pale in comparison to the setting of an evaluation study in which the purpose of the policy being studied is not to learn something but *to do something.* Policymakers under these conditions often have other and, to them, more urgent priorities to take into account than those of researchers. They are unlikely to be moved by arguments that the policy being implemented must be carefully specified, uniform, and sufficiently distinguishable from other policies so as to avoid the research hurdles discussed in chapter 4.

Moreover, there are bound to be important players in the policy process who regard research as an intrusion that can only delay, complicate, or even undercut a policy and its implementation. They may be antagonistic to researchers as a group. Or on political grounds they may not want research to be conducted because they fear it would show a policy they favor to be ineffective or, if it works, to have results that fall short of what had been promised.

As in the case of demonstration research, these political realities, along with the inevitable limitations of resources (both human and fiscal), all point to a role for evaluation research that recognizes its selective character. Not all programs can be the subject of evaluation research, referring here to independent, systematic studies as opposed to the kinds of monitoring and oversight activities often labeled "evaluations" but which are not *research*.

Even when policymakers are sympathetic to the purposes of evaluation research, the differences in perspective between policymakers and researchers are likely to be substantial. The relationship between the two communities is rarely smooth and easy. Unlike social scientists, politicians often regard ambiguity as a good thing. It can enable them to forge a coalition of different interests, each perceiving that its aims have priority. Politicians also tend to deal in small increments of change.

In short, for a number of reasons the process of policymaking is likely to cause policymakers to behave in ways that diverge from the interests and orientation of researchers. For the moment, my point is only that because of these differences social scientists doing evaluation research do not have the same opportunity they have in the case of smaller, focused demonstration studies to control the conditions under which their research is conducted.

Limits in Establishing the Counterfactual State

The most important consequence of the limited control that researchers have in an evaluation study compared to a demonstration study is that it is more difficult to establish the counter-

factual state. Demonstration and evaluation research ask the same bottom-line question: what happened as a result of this policy that would not have happened if the policy being studied did not exist? We can never have a perfect solution, one in which the same person or group is both treated and untreated by a given policy. The next best solution, as we have seen, is to randomly assign a number of eligible persons or groups to treatment and nontreatment groups and to compare the differences between the two groups in terms of the kinds of changes that a given policy is supposed to produce.

However, in a situation where research is a lower-order objective (it may even be opposed by some participants in the policy process), the suggestion that a rigorous design should be adopted to evaluate an ongoing program by randomly excluding some participants from the program is likely to be strongly resisted. There may be situations in which random assignment *should* be resisted in an evaluation study. On ethical grounds, if the policy in question is *universal* (that is, if it applies to all eligible persons, as with the Social Security retirement system or food stamps), one is hard put to argue that the policy should be suspended for some otherwise eligible participants in the interest of science.

As we have already seen, other "less-good" alternatives compared to random assignment exist for establishing the counterfactual state. If the policy we are evaluating is selective (for example, grants are given to some places but not others), one could argue that the government should randomly select some places as comparison sites in order to create a matched sample of nonparticipating persons or organizations for research purposes. Although such an approach may make good sense to researchers, it can involve problems for government officials. They may decide that it is politically unwise to have comparison sites because this would be perceived as unfair. Or government grant officers may not want to provide the funds to set up comparison sites or in some other way collect data on a comparison group.

The discussion of demonstration research in the earlier chapters included simulation techniques to create a comparison group statistically. This is often the favored approach for evaluation studies. This involves predicting a particular set of dependent variables (dependent on the policy being studied) for a population eligible to be aided by the policy but which is not affected by it. Benchmarks based on past research or on the views of experts can also be used as the standards against which to measure the performance of program participants.

Despite the preference of researchers for random assignment for establishing the counterfactual, the fact is that this approach is extremely difficult to bring to bear in evaluating an ongoing government program once it has been adopted. Indeed, none of the evaluation studies of the Great Society programs (for example, Head Start, Follow-Through, Job Corps, compensatory school aid) involved randomly assigned control groups.* Some studies of the Great Society programs, as in the case of the Job Corps evaluation, used comparison sites; most evaluation research on these programs used econometric techniques.

Institutional Impacts

Evaluation research is more likely to focus on institutional impacts as opposed to individual impacts. This third difference can be shown by continuing our example of the computer-assisted remedial reading program used in chapter 4. I stipu-

*The two MDRC evaluation research projects considered in this section on evaluation research, the California work/welfare program and the Job Training Partnership Act (which MDRC conducts jointly with Abt Associates), are the first efforts I know of to use random assignment in an evaluation study of a large-scale ongoing program.

lated there that this was a state demonstration program and showed how it raised policy research questions for school districts and local schools. Let us now assume, as is not unusual in American government, that the federal government has adopted a grant-in-aid program that provides funds to the states for reading remediation. In many states, such aid is usually in addition to grants provided by state governments and local funds for the same purpose. Policymakers in Washington have an interest in the response to *their* program. Thus, their questions are likely to center on the behavior of different levels of government and types of organizations and actors in the political process in response to the new federal grants-in-aid for reading remediation. What do states do with these funds? What do school districts do with them? What do individual schools do? Are they additive? Are computer companies, consultants, experts important actors in the use of these grant funds?

These are impacts. But they are a different type of impacts from those we considered in the case of demonstration studies. These are *institutional impacts* relating to the way different types of governments, organizations, and political actors respond to policy changes. The assessment of these kinds of institutional impacts involves establishing the counterfactual state. What did these institutions, organizations, and actors do that they would not otherwise have done because of the new federal grant program?

This discussion reveals an interesting connection between the two types of studies we are considering. One might argue that demonstration research should focus more on *individual* outcomes. Will a computer-assisted reading remediation program help children learn how to read? If we prove in a demonstration study that such programs have significant positive impacts, then it may be decided to adopt a national program in the form of grant-in-aid from the federal government to the states to foster this objective. However, once we have such a national program, we then will be most interested in whether it changes the behavior of the *institutions* that provide this service. How do state education agencies and local school districts use these funds? Specifically, what kinds of programs, techniques, instructors, and equipment are used? How are programs organized? How much is spent on them? How do they affect the curriculum of schools and the behavior and attitudes of both school personnel and students? The same reasoning and questions apply to state grants-in-aid. Actually, most of the business of providing public services in the domestic public sector in the United States is conducted on this basis through intergovernmental subventions.

A fundamental theoretical point underlies this observation about the potentially greater significance of institutional impacts, as opposed to individual impacts, in evaluation research. Politicians often act by *indirection* to affect the lives of citizens. They seek to change the behavior of *institutions* in the hope or belief that such changes in institutional behavior will influence the services and activities of these institutions in ways that will eventually affect individual citizens.

These institutional and federalism dimensions of evaluation research are often overlooked. Particularly in the United States, federalism is the "barrier reef" of evaluation research. Researchers must watch this reef carefully, for it can ruin their voyages if they do not take it into account. This warning reflects a more general problem. I refer to the lack of understanding of the nature of state and local government on the part of many policymakers in that capital city of easy abstractions—Washington, D.C.—where decisions are all too often made with little knowledge of the great diversity and operational realities of American federalism.

This federalism "reef" affects decisions about policy research in many ways. A policy intervention in the form of a grant-in-aid from one level of government to another, for example, may be relatively small. It may be relatively *so* small that, following the reasoning stated earlier in regard to the null hypothesis, we would not expect to find detectable *individual* impacts of a federal stream of money as opposed to other streams of money from a state government or private citizens. The study of the institutional and intergovernmental impacts in such a context differs from the study of the impacts on individuals of a demonstration program for a small sample under controlled conditions.

These observations on the design and conduct of public policy research underscore the theme of this book about the need for linkages between social science disciplines and between quantitative and qualitative research designs and methods. The kinds of generalizations that political scientists or sociologists make about institutional behavior in response to a given policy change often involve the way different types of organizations and political actors behave. In theory, we could study differences in organizational or political behavior by randomly selecting a sample of a given type of organization (for example, schools, as in the previous illustration), treating them in different ways, and then analyzing their responses to the policy being evaluated in order to generalize about its effects. However, the study of policy effects on institutions does not easily lend itself to experimental research on this basis. What are the reasons for this? In part, it is a reflection of the lack of sufficiently strong and widely agreed-upon theories about organizational and political behavior on which to base a rigorous and sharply focused research design. It is also a reflection of the lack of accepted, measurable variables with which to conduct a detailed analysis of organizational and political behavior even if we do use a formal experimental research design.

Other and more pragmatic factors also come into play here. Organizations are harder to manipulate in a research setting than individuals. Consider the difficulties that would be involved in seeking informed consent from an organization to subject itself to a random-selection procedure that would determine whether or not it would receive some presumed benefit. Many organizations in the American political context are too complex and assertive to participate in this way in applied social science research.

From a methodological point of view, we also need to look at the way researchers deal with causality in studying organizational behavior as opposed to individual behavior. The most common method for studying the behavior of organizations is to observe them closely in order to make *informed judgments* about how a given stimulus or event (for example, a policy change) appears to have affected the behavior of a given set or type of organizations. This is an *inductive* research method. It should be (and often is) systematic, objective, and rigorous—in a word "scientific." What researchers do in such a situation is *model the counterfactual* on the basis of the available facts and experience and their knowledge of organizational behavior. They observe the behavior of an organization or group of organizations under conditions in which a new policy is in effect and compare that behavior to what they predict would have been their behavior without the new policy. The catch, and it is a significant one, is that we cannot specify and tightly replicate this reasoning process.

We need in this context to look at the role of different social science disciplines in public policy research. Since the mid-1960s when academic social scientists and policy analysts emerged as players in governmental decision making, economists have been the dominant actors. While some economists have resisted this movement to be relevant, a substantial number of their colleagues have turned their attention (in some cases their full attention) to applied research. In my view, this is to their credit.

Other disciplines, notably political science, have had their moment on the public policy stage, but have not played as significant a role in recent years. Public administration as a subfield of political science had its heyday in the early part of the century, but since then has been relegated to a relatively low status in the discipline.

Recently, in political science there has been renewed interest in institutional studies. An article by James G. March and Johan P. Olsen calling for "a new institutionalism," which appeared in 1984 in the *American Political Science Review*, stimulated widespread comment and discussion.[4] March and Olsen maintain that because institutions are not the sum of the actions of their members, their behavior is not easily predicted; it is often ahistorical and characterized by symbolic action. They call for greater emphasis in political science on institutional research that takes cognizance of these characteristics of organizational behavior. I believe this is a fortuitous development; political scientists with this kind of a real-world orientation to the study of institutions could make a substantial contribution to public policy evaluation research.

Sociologists also have a good claim on the field of organizational behavior; however, the study of institutional responses to changes in public policy has not been a strong current of research by sociologists. Robert A. Scott and Arnold R. Shore, in a pessimistic book entitled *Why Sociology Does Not Apply*, observe that sociologists, insofar as they have been involved in policy-related research, have done studies to analyze policy problems and prescribe solutions. (These essentially are what were described in the first chapter as studies of conditions and trends.) Scott and Shore conclude that the results of these studies have been disappointing; they are often "politically unrealistic, administratively unworkable, or simply impractical." They also complain that policy-relevant sociological research is too often "stimulated by a desire to advance disciplinary knowledge."[5]

Psychology is another social science discipline with a good claim on the field of organizational behavior, despite the observations by Nathan Kaplan and Stephen D. Nelson that the discipline is characterized by what they call a "person-centered preoccupation." Kaplan and Nelson question whether such a person-centered approach is "a suitable foundation for the development and promulgation of ameliorative programs."[6] On the other hand, Thomas F. Pettigrew, a leader in the field of social psychology, while not optimistic about the amount of change in research practice that can be achieved, reaches conclusions similar to mine. He advocates continued efforts to advance applied social science through the study of organizational behavior, "more interdisciplinary work within social science," and efforts to merge inductive and deductive methods.[7]

Conclusion

The setting for evaluation research as compared to demonstration research is much less amenable to control by researchers and often involves different questions (many of which are scientifically harder to answer) than the questions at the forefront in demonstration studies. The difference in the kinds of questions asked in evaluation research makes the case for multidisciplinary studies even stronger in this area than in demonstration research, although it is strong in both areas. Furthermore, the fact that many of the most critical questions in evaluation research (namely, institutional questions) do not lend themselves to scientific approaches as rigorous as those used in studying the impacts of the tested programs on individuals in demonstration research makes it essential to combine quantitative and qualitative methods and data in evaluation research. These and other differences between demonstration and evaluation research can be illustrated by specific research projects. In the next chapter, the MDRC evaluation study of the statewide California work/welfare program adopted in September 1985 is used as an example.

7

The California
GAIN Program

WHEN POLITICIANS write new laws they are often too absorbed in coalition building and horse trading to worry about the way their new program is going to be implemented. The California Greater Avenues for Independence (GAIN) legislation enacted in September 1985 is an intricate—almost Rube Goldberg-like—balancing act of different legislative interests and concerns on a subject fraught with emotional content. The purpose of the legislation is to convert the administrative system for the AFDC category of welfare recipients from a payment process into a service system of job preparation and work-facilitation in order to reduce welfare dependency. All AFDC family heads whose youngest child is six years of age or older are required to participate in the GAIN program if child care is available; most participants are single women with children. AFDC family heads with children under six years of age can volunteer to participate in the GAIN program in which case they are eligible to receive support services. This includes payments for child care at prevailing rates and for transportation as well as for ancillary work-related expenses such as uniforms, books, and clothing.

The authors of the California GAIN legislation determined that it was necessary to specify each component of the system in the law (often in considerable detail) in order to win and hold political support from a coalition of liberals and conservatives. The two leading players in writing the legislation were David B. Swoap, secretary of California's Health and Welfare Agency, and state Assemblyman Arthur Agnos. Swoap was the principal negotiator for Governor George Deukmejian, a conservative Republican. Previously, Swoap had been the director of welfare in California under Ronald Reagan; he also served in Washington in the Reagan administration as deputy secretary of the Department of Health and Human Services. Swoap's counterpart in the negotiations, Arthur Agnos, is a liberal Democrat who represented San Francisco in the state legislature when the GAIN program was enacted. (Agnos was elected mayor of San Francisco in December 1987.)

Shortly after the GAIN law was enacted, Swoap described the program in terms that highlighted the delicate political balancing act underlying its enactment. He said that the program "incorporates a unique blend of what have traditionally been considered 'liberal' and 'conservative' attitudes towards caring for the poor." Swoap specifically referred to the San Diego work/welfare demonstration conducted by the Manpower Demonstration Research Corporation as having shown the efficacy of this approach: "The seeds of California's reform were planted over the last three years, by the success of San Diego County's Experimental Work Project."[1] The debate on GAIN in the legislature focused on the participation requirement as the key to the political compromise needed to enact the new program. Again according to Swoap, "The opposition of many legislators to the mandatory component began to fade as results from San Diego showed that the overwhelming majority of participants themselves felt the program should be mandatory, because, had it not been, they never would have participated, and acquired valuable training and experience."[2]

Although Swoap, on behalf of the Deukmejian administration, underscored the obligational character of the GAIN program and the link to the San Diego MDRC demonstration, Agnos and other members of the legislature who participated in the policy process had a different set of preferences. They stressed the services provided, and drew heavily on the model of the Massachusetts "E.T. Choices" program sponsored by Governor Michael Dukakis and initiated in October 1983. In this period Dukakis actively publicized his state's program, which involved voluntary participation whereby recipients had a "choice" of the "E.T." (employment and training) services they preferred. A delegation of California officials, including both Swoap and Agnos, visited Massachusetts while the California legislature was working on the GAIN legislation.

The legislation establishing the GAIN program is organized on an elaborate stepwise basis. The detailed description that follows indicates the nature of the research task faced by MDRC in mid-1986 when the corporation entered into a contract with the state to evaluate the GAIN program.

Steps in the GAIN Process

The first step in the GAIN process is registration and orientation. All welfare family heads with children over six years of age are required to register. The second step is appraisal and testing. Participants who pass literacy and skills tests are expected to engage in a job search either on an individual basis or in a group setting in a "job club." In the case of registrants who fail the literacy and skills tests, remedial education or special language training is to be provided at this juncture.

For participants who do not secure employment after the job

search or after they have gone through an educational remediation or English-as-a-second-language program, an individual service plan is to be developed based on the contract signed by a caseworker and the GAIN participant. The contract embodies the *mutual obligation* that is central to the GAIN program. The idea is that the individual recipient agrees to participate in services tailored to her needs and the welfare agency in turn agrees to see to it that these services are provided.

The determination of the types of services most appropriate in a given case is based on a "needs assessment" that is also spelled out in detail in the legislation. After completing the agreed-to services based on the needs assessment, the law prescribes another job search. If a participant is still not employed after this job search, she then can be assigned to a community work-experience project.

Work experience is called PREP in the California GAIN system; the acronym stands for *pre-employment preparation.* There are two types of PREP: "Basic PREP" provides work experience and helps participants obtain references that can assist them in obtaining unsubsidized employment, and "Advanced PREP" enchances job skills.[3] The law stipulates that PREP assignments can be short term, lasting up to three months, or long term, lasting up to one year, and that PREP work assignments cannot exceed thirty-two hours per week. Publications describing the GAIN program include a flow chart showing the steps and branches in the GAIN process just described (see figure 7.1).

The MDRC Evaluation

The MDRC began its evaluation of the GAIN program in March 1986, six months after the enactment of the legislation. The corporation's initial report on the planning and early im-

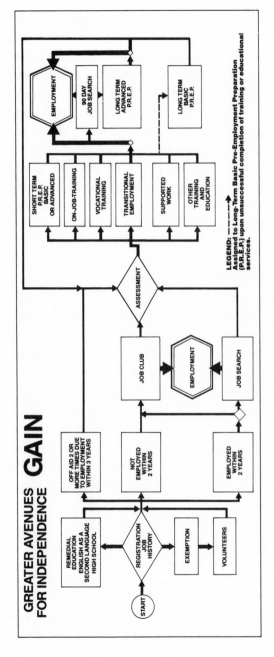

FIGURE 7.1

GAIN Flow Chart

Source: State of California, *GAIN Participant's Manual,* sec. 4, p. 5.

plementation of the GAIN program was issued one year later, in April 1987. It characterizes the new program as "one of the broadest arrays of services and support ever offered in a welfare employment program." The implementation process involves literally thousands of agencies and organizations at the state and county levels. The lead role assigned to the state's Department of Social Services is "to harness the resources and expertise available from the community colleges, adult schools, regional occupational centers and programs, child care agencies, Job Training and Partnership Act (JTPA) programs, and the local offices of the employment services (administered by the Employment Development Department in California)."[4] The MDRC's first report identified four main features that distinguish the GAIN program: (1) its wide array of services; (2) the mandate to participate, projected to involve more than 200,000 welfare family heads by 1990; (3) the individualized character of participation; and (4) the continuous nature of the participation process.

The fourth feature of the GAIN program, the requirement that it be operated as a continuous process without an unassigned pool of registrants, is a major departure from past practice. In most states, there has always been a large "holding" category under the Work Incentives Program (WIN), the federal grant-in-aid that provides funds to the states to support employment and training services to welfare family heads. The continuous and obligational character of the GAIN process has important implications for welfare policy. Referring to this commitment to serve all eligible participants until they have exited from AFDC, the MDRC early-implementation report noted that "welfare payments to this portion of the caseload would no longer be an unconditional entitlement, but become, instead, a *reciprocal obligation.*"[5] When the GAIN program was enacted, it was projected that when it was fully operational the program would cost $335 million per year. This is almost as much spending for employment and training services associated with AFDC in California as there had been for the whole country under the WIN program at the peak level of its spending. (Spending under the GAIN program so far, in 1988—its second year of operation—has already exceeded the original $335 million figure.)

Adding to the challenge of implementing the ambitious goals embodied in the GAIN legislation is an important federalism dimension as discussed in chapter 6. The AFDC program in California is administered by *county* governments. There are fifty-eight counties in California, ranging in population from Los Angeles with 8.2 million people, the largest county in the nation, to rural Alpine County, in northern California, with 1,180 people. The law setting up the program gave counties two years to develop their plans for GAIN, which are subject to review and approval by the state. The overall goal is to have the full state AFDC caseload phased into GAIN over the five-year period from 1985 to 1990. The initial MDRC report on GAIN was completed as the first nine counties were beginning to participate in the program. The authors of this report found the state Department of Social Services to be taking a "strong leadership role." They also found "broad support" for the program and enthusiasm on the part of county welfare directors "about playing a leadership role that could reduce the stigma attached to both welfare agencies and recipients." However, despite these early positive indicators, the initial report indicated that the participating counties had discovered the planning process to be "far more complex, demanding, and time-consuming than originally envisioned."[6]

The Research Challenge

At this writing, the implementation of the GAIN program has been under way for two years. My purpose here is to describe the planning and initiation of the MDRC evaluation and to assess its significance in terms of the ideas presented in this book about the conduct of public policy research. Even by mid-1987, the lessons from this research provided rich case study material. By this time, it was clear that the observation made in the previous chapter about implementation being an exploration and discovery process applied in this instance. The statute establishing the GAIN program indicated the way the program was "supposed" to work. But is this what will actually happen? Will the prescribed services be provided on an interconnected and sequential basis that eventually reaches all of the intended participants?

In its earlier demonstration studies, MDRC collected what researchers refer to as "process data" to understand the "black box" of program operation. But for the GAIN study this part of the task was different; the early phase of the research was exclusively an implementation or process study. It was not possible, as in the smaller confines and more controlled setting of a demonstration study, to immediately undertake structured research on individual program impacts. A study of the impact of the GAIN program on individual participants is a major component of the overall research design developed by state officials in consultation with MDRC; in fact, the individual impact study is regarded by many state officials as the ultimate test of the effectiveness of the GAIN program. My point in this case applies to timing. In this kind of setting, the beginning of the evaluation research process requires an essentially inductive, qualitative approach to study the institutional effects of the GAIN program.

As suggested earlier, I believe that these differences between the GAIN research and the earlier MDRC demonstration studies are not just differences in degree, but differences in kind. Large government programs that are worth learning about through public policy research almost always involve complex political processes and administrative arrangements. They are subject to considerable discretion and differences of interpretation in different locales. As such a program moves into operation, there are bound to be surprises. Eventually, as programs are put into practice and are better understood, research can become more specific and more highly structured. Under GAIN, for example, as more is known about the shape and character of the program, researchers can use a more formal research design to gauge the impact of GAIN services on individual program participants.

The Systems Approach to Public Policy Research

In essence, the MDRC's research on the work/welfare approach to the reform of the AFDC program in California involved a *two-stage* process. In the first stage, a relatively small-scale demonstration research project in one county in California was used as one way to decide what should and, indeed, what could be done to reform California's welfare system. In the second stage, the broader evaluation study, MDRC's task is to study whether and how a new program, once it has been adopted, is implemented on a large scale. This discussion compresses much research history. Some of the earlier MDRC work/welfare studies—notably in West Virginia and Virginia—involved broad-gauged programs operating on a statewide basis, although the MDRC research in these cases concentrated on a limited number of sites. Moreover, it needs to be emphasized that the decision to enact the GAIN program was based on other inputs besides research results, most particularly the goals and values of decision makers as well as those of their constituents.

Despite the fact that the distinction between demonstration and evaluation studies is not hard and fast, taken together the two types of applied social science studies in this case can be seen as *an agent for institutional change.* Demonstration studies helped public officials to decide what they should do and how they could do it to transform the welfare system into a system that emphasizes work and job preparation. Once the GAIN program was adopted, evaluation research enabled public officials to assess both the implementation and the impact on individuals of this new public policy.

This point about viewing demonstration studies and evaluation research on a combined basis as an agent for institutional change is based on the idea, described in chapter 6, that the political and research terrains differ when we move from demonstration to evaluation research. The task of ascertaining the impact of a program on individual participants may be a key part of the research process in an evaluation study, as is true in the case of the evaluation research for the GAIN program, but, in contrast to a demonstration research project, we need to know more about whether and how institutional change takes place before we can study its impact on individuals.

Institutional change in this instance has several dimensions. One is the political and organizational dimension: do the agencies that are to carry out the changed objectives of the new GAIN program actually do so in a way that resembles what was envisioned in the legislation? There is also a psychological dimension: does the behavior of the people in the agency and the recipients of welfare benefits change in the way it was expected to change? Do the key groups in the state welfare bureaucracy make clear what is now expected of welfare recipients and do the recipients understand and accept these new expectations?

These political, organizational, and attitudinal dimensions of policy implementation concern social science disciplines other than economics. Political scientists, psychologists, and sociologists are essential to effective evaluation research, which responds to what politicians want and need to learn about how to change the provision of public services. Economists, as has been stressed throughout, deserve credit for taking a leadership role in policy research. Nevertheless, my concern is that their contribution has skewed our thinking in a way that can limit the role of policy research in the governmental process. We need a broader approach.

The California GAIN evaluation by MDRC is a good illustration of what I mean. The research design for the GAIN program includes "other" (that is, other than economics) research dimensions. The design for this study includes an institutional component that examines the implementation process, an analysis of the way that participants progress through major services, and an evaluation of staff and recipient attitudes toward the GAIN process and program. It also includes a research component centered on individual impacts similar to MDRC's earlier work/welfare demonstration studies. The challenge of the research plan for the GAIN program is to integrate these elements.

At this juncture we need to examine the structure and steps of the GAIN evaluation. The full research menu—institutional impacts, participant progress through the system, staff and individual participants' attitudes, individual impacts, and the cost-benefit analysis—will be conducted in six to eight counties designated as "Tier I" counties. Another group of six to ten "Tier II" counties will be the subject of all but the individual impact part of the study. Aggregate data will be collected for the rest of the counties in the state. The individual impact study with random assignment is projected to involve approximately 12,000 people in the Tier I counties.

The institutional portion of the GAIN study will be based on interview and program data. The bulk of the interviews will survey administrators in county welfare departments. A smaller number of interviews will survey the staffs of education, training, and child-care organizations, as well as other service providers. The MDRC staff members work with sociologists, social psychologists, and political scientists who specialize in organizational behavior and program management in the design and execution of these parts of the research. The study of participant progress through the GAIN system will be based primarily on such factors as the type and length of service provided and program content. Initially it was hoped that there would be a uniform statewide data system on the status and services of all GAIN participants. However, efforts to bring this about came up against the long-standing commitment on the part of county officials to local program control. This lack of a single, central, and uniform GAIN data system, which both state officials and the MDRC researchers had hoped to avoid, represents a substantial evaluation research hurdle. The result is the need to set up individualized data systems in each of the Tier I and Tier II counties for the GAIN study.

An important component of the GAIN study is the survey research on the effects of the GAIN program on the attitudes of agency staff and welfare recipients. The aim of the GAIN program, and of the similar work/welfare programs being implemented in other states, is to convert welfare from a payment system into a system that focuses on job preparation, employment, and the reduction of dependency. The hope is that the behavior of the bureaucracy will change, that agency employees will transmit new signals to welfare recipients, and that in turn this will affect the attitudes and expectations of GAIN participants. As part of the research team for the GAIN study,

MDRC is working with experts on attitudinal research to survey the staff members of county welfare and related social service agencies on how they view the GAIN program and how, if at all, their attitudes toward their job and toward welfare recipients have been influenced by the new program. Each interview, approximately one hour long, includes closed-ended and open-ended questions. The survey of registrants' attitudes focuses on perceptions of the program's fairness and helpfulness; it also examines the program's effects on "self-perception."

These three components of the institutional research (the implementation, participant flow, and attitudinal studies) have been designed to reinforce each other. The survey research on the attitudes of welfare agency personnel, for example, includes questions about the tasks performed (how they are conducted and viewed), which will be a valuable supplement to the data collected on implementation and managerial processes under GAIN.

Discoveries in the Implementation Process

Findings from the GAIN evaluation research already under way (the full study is projected to be completed in mid-1991) confirm that implementation is a discovery process. Education is a good example: in the planning process for GAIN, state officials estimated that one-quarter of the participants would need remedial education. However, as the first counties began the GAIN program, it became apparent that these early estimates were substantially wrong. This discovery was made in the development of test instruments for GAIN.

Literacy and skills testing, as noted, is an early step in the GAIN process. Examinations are administered to all partici-

pants. Test instruments were developed by the California Departments of Education and Social Services early in 1986. Pilot
tests were administered in five counties. Altogether 6,331 people participated in these tests between July and December
1986. A report on these pilot tests was issued in April 1987; it
indicated that 57 percent of the people who took these tests
required some form of remediation in literacy or arithmetic
skills.

The purpose of these pilot tests was to validate the exams
used. According to the director of the Department of Social
Services, Linda S. McMahon, the results of the pilot tests
showed that the "testing instruments selected will perform
successfully."[7] Neither this departmental statement nor the
longer report released to the press at the time commented on
the size of the group that required remediation. However,
newspapers published the results, not as a validation of the test,
but as an indication of the seriousness of the problem of inadequate literacy and arithmetic skills on the part of welfare family
heads. In one newspaper account of the results, the official in
charge of the initiation of the GAIN program, Carl Williams,
spoke about the policy significance of these results: "The mes-
sage is pretty clear that we have one heck of a population out
there that's in need of remediation." He added, "The welfare
system is a holding area for people who did not get a good
enough education."[8] This was no surprise to experts in the field
or to people who follow social policy issues closely. Gordon
Berlin and Andrew Sum, for example, have described "the
basic skills crisis" as the single most important national social
problem. "Inadequate basic skills—the ability to read, write,
compute, and communicate—is a common thread running
throughout the web of social problems."[9]

This publication of the scores from the test evaluation had
a ripple effect throughout the GAIN system. At the highest
levels, it caused concern in the legislature, particularly among

conservative members who had supported GAIN and were worried about the cost implications of these test results. This political sensitivity is by no means special. A synergism is involved here, whereby major public programs in sensitive areas are constantly subject to scrutiny and adjustment. As it turned out, the ultimate effect of this controversy about test scores was good for the GAIN program; an additional appropriation of $41 million was provided, with support from Governor Deukmejian, for remedial education.

This test scores incident demonstrates how important schools are in the institutional change process of the GAIN program. This linkage was proving to be most challenging at precisely the time that remedial education was found to be even more critical than originally anticipated. The GAIN law requires that in counties in which there are unused funds allocated to local school districts under the state's education aid program, these slots should be used for remediation under GAIN. On the surface this is appealing. Rather than appropriating new funds for remedial education, the state and counties should make use of available funds already allocated to school districts but not yet appropriated at the local level. The catch is that the schools are a strong, deeply rooted public institution not used to serving adult welfare recipients.

Timing factors are crucial in knitting together the welfare system and the schools. Schools operate on a September-to-June calendar. Some GAIN participants who are referred to local public schools toward the end of the school year (for example, in March or April) for remedial education may be told that class space will not be available until September. This defeats the idea of continuous service with no unassigned pool of participants. A thirty-year-old welfare mother is unlikely to believe (and understandably so) that GAIN is a new regime involving a serious and active commitment to her future if she is told that there will be a five-month delay between her first exposure to the program and the beginning of service.

In Santa Clara County, one of the first urbanized counties to enter the GAIN program, the press reported that the failure rate for the literacy and skills test was very high, 76 percent. The problem of integrating the school and welfare systems was brought to light in an early press account of one recipient's experience:

> Nancy, a 37-year old mother of three boys who has been on welfare for five years, said she has refused to join the workfare program because of her job experience. The San Jose woman, who said she has been a waitress and a candy store clerk, asked that her last name not be used because she feared that her welfare check would be cut off.
>
> "I went down one day, and they had an (orientation) class for me," she said. "Then I was supposed to see a social worker a few days later. But no one called me for about three weeks. When they finally called they said I had to learn how to read and write better to get a job.
>
> "Listen," she said. "I've worked before. I have three sons. I haven't been to school since I was 15. It's too late for me to learn, but no one down there will listen to me. I can work; I know I can. But they say they have their rules and that's that."[10]

Other discoveries made in the GAIN start-up process provide useful, although not always appreciated, lessons about the program terrain. The MDRC report on early implementation, for example, uncovered a problem of "no shows" when welfare family heads were referred to the GAIN program. The report described these lower-than-anticipated enrollment levels: "In some cases it was 40 to 80 percent below projections early on, and as high as 25 to 50 percent after several months of operation."[11] Some explanations for this situation are obvious. In the past, requirements that welfare family heads show up for counseling and service programs (and there have been such requirements in the law for a long time) were not observed and both local welfare workers and recipients knew this to be the case. Now, under the new program, welfare workers are told to refer recipients to the GAIN program, and that attendance is required. The workers may not be convinced that this requirement is serious, or for some other reason they may not make this feature of the GAIN system clear to welfare recipients.

In sum, it is extremely difficult to change the behavior of both providers and recipients in a large public service bureaucracy. Attention to and acceptance of the changed signal (people must work or be trained) means that ingrained attitudes and behavior patterns must be reversed in the people who process and in the people who receive welfare benefits. It is already evident in California, as in other states implementing new work/welfare programs under similar conditions, that major efforts are required to change these deep-seated attitudes. Passing a law is only the beginning.

What happened in the case of the schools is an early and publicized example of the kinds of discoveries in the implementation process that are critical to an assessment of the GAIN program. The point is not that GAIN is unique, but that any large-scale public program is bound to take its shape in the discovery process of implementation and furthermore that its character will probably vary from one location to the next.

The essential questions for government are twofold: once we decide what we want to do to change the welfare system, can we make it happen and will it work? The MDRC conducted work/welfare demonstrations on an issue that politicians care about (linking work and welfare) which have already provided valuable information about the challenge of these strategies as a starting point for evaluation research.

To conclude this chapter on research in process, I offer several comments on the cumulative effect of the MDRC studies in the welfare field. Although I have been a close observer of this research, I have not been directly involved in conducting it. As I view the learning curve of this research since the national supported-work demonstration, I am impressed that these studies involve more than a series of individual research projects. Taken together, they provide a substantial knowledge base about the nature and workings of welfare systems and the policy process and political issues that are important in this field. Based on this experience, the researchers have come to have a teaching function, which in the case of the work/welfare studies has already had a significant impact in the national policy process. The cumulative results of these linked policy research studies exceed what could have been anticipated when the first steps were taken to initiate the supported-work demonstration in the mid-1970s.

8

Field Network
Evaluation Studies

DONALD T. CAMPBELL and Thomas D. Cook draw a distinction similar to the one used in this book between situations in which the experimental approach (random assignment to treatment and control groups) is the most desirable research method and those in which other approaches are more appropriate.

> The advantages of experimental control for inferring causation have to be weighed against the disadvantages that arise because we do not always want to know about causation in controlled settings. Instead, for many purposes, we would like to be able to generalize to causal relationships in complex field settings, and we cannot easily assume that findings from the laboratory will hold up in the field.[1]

Much of my own experience as a researcher has been devoted to the second task described by Campbell and Cook, "generalizing to causal relationships in complex field settings." Specifically, this research evaluates the effects on state and local governments of major changes in the grant-in-aid policies and programs of the federal government, especially in situations in which the federal government through grants-in-aid seeks to influence the behavior of states and localities.

This chapter describes the research methodology developed by an interdisciplinary group of social science researchers, based initially at the Brookings Institution, to study the effects of a series of major federal grant-in-aid programs, beginning with revenue sharing. In chapter 7 we looked at the state-local relationship in the GAIN program; in this chapter we consider the relationships between the federal government and the governments of states and localities.

Federal revenue sharing was enacted in 1972 under President Nixon to provide general-purpose grants ($5.3 billion per annum in the initial period) to state governments and some 39,000 city, county, and township governments. I was involved in the design and enactment of revenue sharing as assistant director of the Office of Management and Budget during the Nixon administration. I had previously been chairman of the transition task force for President-elect Nixon in 1968 that recommended a revenue sharing program to the new administration. After serving in government for four years during the first term of the Nixon administration, I returned to the Brookings Institution as a member of the research staff of the Governmental Affairs program.

The Revenue Sharing Program

Revenue sharing was the keystone of Nixon's New Federalism. The revenue sharing program, in existence from 1972 until it was ended under the Reagan administration in 1986, was a multipurpose program. Altogether, over fourteen years, the revenue sharing program paid out nearly $80 billion. However, only Gerald Ford, among Nixon's successors, strongly supported this program. Neither Carter nor Reagan shared Nixon's enthusiasm for the revenue sharing program. Under Carter, state governments were eliminated as recipients, and under Reagan the remaining payments to local governments (two-thirds of the original total) were ended.

When it was enacted in 1972 supporters of the revenue sharing program backed it for different reasons. Some saw it, as I believe Nixon did, primarily as an instrument of decentralization. Nixon frequently complained, using conventional Republican rhetoric, about the excessive fragmentation and complexity of the federal grant-in-aid system with its hundreds (the counts differed) of so-called categorical grant-in-aid programs that were seen as undermining the priority-setting processes of state and local governments and weakening their role vis-à-vis what was perceived as the growing and increasingly intrusive role of the national government in domestic affairs. Many Democrats, too, criticized the growing rigidities of categorical federal grant-in-aid programs in this period. Walter Heller, a Democrat who supported revenue sharing as chairman of the Council of Economic Advisors in the Johnson administration and urged Johnson to adopt this idea, referred to the existing grant system as suffering from "hardening of the categories." The answer to this problem, especially for middle-of-the-road Republicans like Nixon, was to change the form of federal grants by adopting grant-broadening initiatives such as revenue sharing and block grants. Revenue sharing, as already noted, means essentially unrestricted grants-in-aid to state and local governments. Block grants are flexible grants allocated on a formula-distribution basis for a broad functional area; they can be used on a discretionary basis by the recipient state and local governments within the aided functional area.

Nixon first proposed revenue sharing in 1969 at the relatively meager (by Washington standards) level of $500 million per year. This amount was not large enough to get Congress's attention. Then in January 1971, in a State of the Union message devoted almost exclusively to domestic affairs, Nixon proposed an $11 billion combined program of revenue sharing and block grants, which included $5 billion per year for revenue sharing and $6 billion in block grants. (Federal spending for grants to states and localities at this time was $34 billion; total federal spending was $231 billion.) Nixon told Congress that the new funds in his federal aid initiatives would increase federal aid by 25 percent. "The time has come," he said, "to reverse the flow of power and responsibilities from the States and communities to Washington, and start power and resources flowing from Washington to States and localities and, more important, to the people, all across America. . . . I reject the patronizing idea that government in Washington, D.C., is inevitably more wise, more honest and more efficient than government at the state and local level." Most of the funds for Nixon's proposed new block grants were obtained by consolidating existing categorical grants into broader programs with some additional funds added, called "sweeteners." Nixon's two most important proposals for block grants, both of which were eventually enacted into law, were for employment and training and for community development.

Unlike the earlier revenue sharing plan he put forward in 1969, Nixon's new, enriched $5 billion per year version of revenue sharing proposed in January 1971 did receive the attention of Congress. It activated state and local officials to lobby seriously for this presidential initiative. In 1972, in the midst of Nixon's reelection campaign, revenue sharing was enacted into law. The President journeyed to Philadelphia to sign the law in the presence of a large group of state and local government officials. At the signing ceremony, Nixon expressed the hope that revenue sharing would "renew" the

American federal system created in Philadelphia two centuries earlier.

Soon after this legislation was enacted, officials of the Ford Foundation approached the Brookings Institution with a proposal that the Brookings Institution consider doing an evaluation study of this new program. It is useful to look at the questions researchers faced in taking up this challenge. The key question asked, What difference did it make to have this new and more flexible fiscal flow from the national government to states and localities? The Brookings Institution formed a research team that I directed to consider this question. From the outset, we decided that an evaluation of the revenue sharing program should focus on two main types of effects of the new program: (1) those that emerged as the *most prominent* effects in the implementation of revenue sharing; and (2) those effects (whether prominent or not) that were *important to politicians* because they were reflected in the major goals of the new program.

This second type of effect is particularly hard to deal with in a research setting. In textbooks on public policy research, we are often told that the first step in an evaluation study is to define a program's objectives. Yet in the case of revenue sharing, as in many other cases, there was little agreement on the goals of the program. The question that researchers must ask is, On what basis should one appraise the success—or failure—of the revenue sharing program?

In addition to Nixon's emphasis on decentralization, other supporters of the program stressed its role in achieving a number of competing, even conflicting, purposes. Among the other goals of revenue sharing were the following: providing fiscal relief to local governments; equalizing fiscal capacity among states and localities; providing new funds to deal with important public sector needs; serving as a stimulus to "innovation" on the part of the recipient state and local governments; stabilizing and reducing state and local taxes, particularly the property tax; and altering the nation's overall tax system by putting more emphasis on income taxation (predominantly federal) as opposed to property and sales taxes. Which of these objectives should be featured in an evaluation study; how should they be weighted? The same people emphasized different policy objectives at different times. Moreover, even if one could have assigned weights to all of the major goals of revenue sharing on the basis of the legislative debates, this would not necessarily have been decisive. The ultimate decision about the success or failure of the program depends on the way these goals are regarded by a particular person or group viewing the effects of the program. Yet, despite the difficulties of the task, a program as large and controversial as revenue sharing surely warrants evaluation research to explain its operation and effects.

Two other important factors complicated the evaluation research in the case of revenue sharing. One was the fact that the program was *universal*. Every state and 39,000 local governments received a share of these funds according to a distribution formula based on Census Bureau statistics for major characteristics of the recipient jurisdictions. There was no way to use some states and cities that did not receive revenue sharing funds as a comparison group for this research.

Compounding the challenge was the "federalism barrier reef." Tremendous variation exists in the structure of the state and local governments that received shared revenue and in the ways that these state and local jurisdictions define and carry out their functions and keep their financial accounts. These conditions reflect a cardinal characteristic of American federalism, its diversity. This characteristic of the U.S. governmental system makes it difficult, to say the least, to conduct evaluation research on federal grant-in-aid programs.

The Research Approach

The Brookings Institution decided to base its evaluation research on revenue sharing on *parallel, uniformly structured case studies of a representative sample of state and local governments.* This field research was conducted by an interdisciplinary group of on-the-scene academic social scientists. Political scientists and economists in roughly equal numbers participated as field researchers. Altogether, twenty-seven field researchers were selected on the basis of their familiarity with this kind of research and with the programs, politics, and finances of the jurisdictions they were studying. (One requirement was that the field researchers have no official connection with the governments they were studying.)

The first step in the research process was to define the types of effects of the revenue sharing program to be studied. Broad categories rather than specifically defined objectives were used to avoid forcing the program into a mold that would reflect the purposes favored by researchers rather than the broad, shifting, and varied aims of supporters of the program. Four categories of effects—fiscal, programmatic, institutional, and distributional—were defined:

1. *Fiscal effects:* the first-order impacts of the revenue sharing program on the finances of the recipient juridictions, particularly the distinction between new spending and substitutive uses of shared revenue.
2. *Programmatic effects:* the types (operating, capital, functional areas) of new spending uses of shared revenue.
3. *Institutional effects:* the impacts of the new program on the decision processes and roles and relationships of the major organizations and actors in the political system of the recipient jurisdictions.
4. *Distributional effects:* the way the national allocation system worked for allocating shared revenue to states and localities.[2]

The distributional effects of revenue sharing (category 4), were studied centrally at the Brookings Institution with demographic and financial data from the Bureau of the Census and program data from the Department of the Treasury, which was responsible for administering the revenue sharing program. Were revenue sharing funds allocated in a way that redistributed these funds according to the relative needs (that is, on an equalization basis) of the recipient jurisdiction? If so, how and to what degree did the program have a *targeting,* as opposed to a *spreading,* effect on the nation's intergovernmental finances?

The determination of the three other types of effects just listed (fiscal, programmatic, and institutional) was made by the researchers in the field. They spent on average thirty days for each of the three rounds of field observations for this evaluation study. Before each round, they participated in a conference at the Brookings Institution, where the central staff and field researchers discussed the conceptual framework and research plan for that round of field observations. The aim was to have all of the members of the field research group agree on the aims and methods of the research and operate on the same "wavelength" in conducting the research.

The field researchers submitted a report for each round of observations. These reports consisted of their answers to both closed-ended and open-ended questions according to a standard reporting format. Field researchers drew on state and local financial and program records and reports by governmental agencies and private organizations; they also interviewed key participants in the decision processes for the state and local allocation of revenue sharing funds. The analysis of the effects of the revenue sharing was done by the field researchers. It was not based on the answers to closed-ended survey questions on the part of the state and local officials interviewed in the field, although other studies of the program took this approach. The

Brookings central staff for this field network evaluation study (myself, two other senior researchers, and a research assistant) reviewed and combined the data and analyses submitted by the field researchers and prepared the overall research reports. These reports were then circulated in draft form for comments to the full research group (all the field researchers) as well as to other experts.

The field sample for this study included sixty-five jurisdictions that received revenue sharing funds—eight state governments, twenty-nine municipalities, twenty-one counties, six townships, and one Indian reservation. The sample overrepresented the larger jurisdictions. It accounted for approximately 20 percent of total program funding. The research was longitudinal. It began soon after the first revenue sharing checks were distributed and continued for six years. The research was supported primarily by grants from the Ford Foundation.

Other studies of the program were also conducted, several of them under the auspices of the National Science Foundation (which also provided partial support for the Brookings research) and by the U.S. General Accounting Office.[3] Two other approaches were used in the evaluation studies of revenue sharing: (1) surveys of state and local officials where the findings of the research consisted of compilations of the answers they provided; and (2) statistical studies that compared the post-revenue sharing experience with the counterfactual state, which was established through econometric modeling.

Researchers in all three camps, as might be expected, had strong opinions about the weaknesses of any approach other than their own. I am no exception. I have substantial reservations about the use of self-reporting survey data in this kind of setting. State and local officials have many options in what they can report about their use of revenue sharing funds. They are likely to tell researchers what they think Congress or their constituency wants to hear, whether or not it represents the way the revenue sharing funds actually affected the finances of their government. The government reports on the revenue sharing program issued by the Department of the Treasury suffered from this problem. The Brookings study combined two methods—the field research and statistical approaches—in an attempt to determine the net effect of this new flow of general-support payments from the federal government to states and localities. However, before describing how the two approaches were combined, it is necessary to say more about the field studies, the main approach used in the Brookings evaluation of the revenue sharing program.

The decision to start the field research at the very outset of the program turned out to be fortuitous. Although there was, as usual, a temptation to devote more time to research design, we expected that the period in which the initial payments of revenue sharing funds were made would be the time that the decision processes for the use of revenue sharing funds would be most prominent and hence easiest to study. The experience of this study and similar field network evaluation studies of other grant-in-aid programs confirmed this assumption.

The purpose of the evaluation study was twofold, to trace and analyze the use of shared revenue and to generalize about its effects on the recipient state and local governments. Although the focus was on institutions (that is, the recipient state and local governments), as opposed to individual citizens as in the case of the demonstration studies described in chapters 3 through 5, the essential research challenge was the same. We needed to model the counterfactual to determine what would have happened in the absence of revenue sharing so that we could draw conclusions about the effects of this new form of federal grants-in-aid. The impact analysis in this case was done by the field researchers. Both the evaluation research and the program being studied were *decentralized.* Field researchers submitted their analytical findings, which in effect were their "judgments" about the impact of shared revenue, to the central staff at the Brookings Institution.

In essence, the field researchers modeled the counterfactual state in that most powerful of all computers, the human brain. This modeling process used many variables, often in elaborate ways. But the process cannot be replicated with statistical procedures to establish a level of confidence in these assessments of causality—the cause being the new revenue sharing program to which we attributed the effects reported in our study.

The central staff reviewed each field report. We did not, however, change the assessments made by the field researchers without consulting with them about the reasons for modifying their findings. In most cases, collegial relationships developed; the role of the central staff was understood to entail eliciting the reasoning behind the analyses made in the field about the effects of revenue sharing and to make certain, to the best of our ability, that the field researchers were using similar approaches, concepts, and definitions across the sample jurisdictions. Other methods were used for checking the field analyses. One such check involved changes in the assignments of the researchers. In some instances, field researchers moved or were unable to continue to work on this study (in two cases field researchers died during the research period). Transfers of responsibility for the field research provided a check on both the research findings and the basic research approach.

Mention was made earlier of the competition among researchers in getting at the elusive question of the impact of the revenue sharing program. Our use of the field network evaluation approach was based on what I would argue are sound scientific notions about the nature of the terrain and the quality of the available data. One cannot unravel the state and local decision process about the use of this new subvention without assembling and analyzing data in the field that are more detailed than the data on state and local finances available centrally from the Bureau of the Census. This is not to denigrate the Census Bureau—I simply want to make the point that their national data on state and local finances are aggregated at a very high level, and even then they are not always comparable in the way programs, revenues, and fiscal accounts are classified and the time periods used for recording them.

To study the impact at the *margin* of a program like revenue sharing, we need a more sensitive data-gathering approach that permits researchers to tailor data collected locally to the question at hand. Again, it is the character of American federalism that makes this so—its diversity, fragmentation, and the strong sense of independence states and localities have about the way they conduct their affairs. This does not mean that other research methods are ruled out. On the contrary, we found that an effective linkage could be made between the field network evaluation methodology and the statistical method. I refer to this as the *complementarity approach*, combining field and statistical methods on a reinforcing basis.

In addition to the field research, later on, when statistical data became available on state and local finances for the period during which we conducted this research, a group of the field researchers undertook a statistical analysis of the fiscal effects of the revenue sharing program. This was done to compare the findings from the field research with the results of this statistical analysis. The two research methods were connected. The knowledge obtained in the field of the workings and institutional setting of the revenue sharing program enabled the researchers for the statistical analysis to design a study that took into account the nature and limitations of the national data on state and local finances.

In the research literature, this strategy of using different methods to study the same question is referred to as "triangulation." The method we adopted for a complementary statistical analysis used regression equations to compare revenue and expenditure patterns before and after revenue sharing to derive inferences about the uses of revenue sharing funds. Observations from the field research guided the design of this analysis. As it turned out, the complementary statistical study of the fiscal effects of shared revenue, which was limited to major cities because of data availability, produced findings in line with those of the field research.[4]

Another point about the relative advantages of using these two approaches to study the impact of revenue sharing concerns the timing and politics of program evaluation. Statistical studies of new national programs like revenue sharing, even under the best of circumstances, typically involve a substantial time lag simply to wait for the requisite data to become available. This may mean that research results will not be timely in terms of the interests and concerns of policymakers or, more important, in relation to the cycle for legislative review and reauthorization. These and other timing considerations had a significant bearing on the revenue sharing evaluation study conducted at the Brookings Institution. Our reports on the field network evaluation study of the revenue sharing program were published in the form of books.[5] We also wrote articles and papers on this research and presented statements and testimony on our findings for audiences such as congressional committees, federal agencies, state and local officials, and the major affected interest groups. The findings were presented according to the four-part framework described earlier for classifying the effects of shared revenue payments—fiscal, programmatic, institutional, and distributional.

The first book on the field network evaluation study of the revenue sharing program was published in January 1975. The original revenue sharing law expired at the end of 1975, so the congressional renewal process was just under way as the research findings became available. In the House, hearings before

the Committee on Governmental Operations (which had jurisdiction over the revenue sharing program) began in June 1974.
In the Senate (where jurisdiction for this program was assigned
to the Finance Committee) hearings were held in April of the
following year. The authors of the Brookings book on this
evaluation study testified at both hearings. In the House, we
previewed our findings because the hearings were held as the
final stages of review and editing were being completed on the
first book on the findings of this research. By the time the
Senate hearings began, this book was available as the basis for
testimony. Under the terms of the grant from the Ford Foundation for this research, copies of this book were sent to all
members of the Congress and other key participants in the
policy process for this program.

Use of Research Findings

To fill in this picture, one needs to step back and reflect on
the position of members of Congress in relation to a program
like revenue sharing. Members of Congress serve on a number
of different committees and subcommittees, each with many
complex matters under its purview. In addition, members have
a wide range of other interests. Their staffs are often overex-
tended in their coverage of policy issues and constituent matters. Moreover, congressional staff members usually do not
have detailed knowledge of specific programmatic issues like
the workings of the revenue sharing program. For this reason,
congressional hearings often serve the dual purpose of a seminar and a political platform. Members of Congress on a committee with substantial responsibility for a program like revenue sharing first need basic facts. What are the salient facts
about this program? How does it affect their critical interests,

region, and major constituencies? As hearings proceed and the subject matter becomes more familiar, hearings can be used less for educational purposes and more for political purposes. Once members have learned about the policy terrain, they can identify their interests, form their views, and stake out their own positions, testing ways to show their support or opposition for a particular program.

The revenue sharing program has unusual qualities in this respect. As a general rule, members of Congress prefer categorical grants (that is, grants for defined and easily dramatized purposes) whereby they can "bring home the bacon," announcing each of their successes in doing so in the local press. Revenue sharing, on the other hand, was seen by Nixon and his chief aides (notably John Ehrlichman and Arthur F. Burns), and others who approved of its decentralizing purposes, as a way to reduce the influence of the national government and to provide greater discretion to the officials of state and local governments "closer to the people." One would expect members of Congress to resist this shift, and on the whole they did. In my view, this was the major reason that revenue sharing (somewhat unusual for federal government programs) died and was buried during Ronald Reagan's presidency.

But for the members of the congressional committees responsible for this legislation, the political scene had a different character; they reaped considerable rewards from supporting revenue sharing. This fact was notable in the political equation of the renewal hearings on revenue sharing. The educational process that occurred at these hearings is clearer in retrospect than it was at the time. Revenue sharing had been enacted four years earlier. The money had been flowing out to states and localities regularly since then. There was some coverage in the press of the payments of shared revenue and in some cases of state and local decisions related to the uses of these funds. But busy members of Congress did not closely follow these events;

it was part of the background of governmental operations, even in the case of members of the committees responsible for revenue sharing legislation. Now the issue was on a front burner. What is it all about? How does the program work? How should they think about and assess the uses of the nearly $20 billion in revenue sharing funds that had been distributed to 39,000 recipient state and local governments at the time the program came up for its first renewal?

The Brookings researchers had answers—answers we had tested in the academic review process by submitting our work for comments to experts on domestic policy and finance. One major issue that emerged early in the discussion of the effects of revenue sharing involved the *fungibility* of revenue sharing dollars; they are very hard to trace. The law required that these funds be assigned to certain broad spending categories named in the law (for example, public safety, environmental protection, transportation, health, social services, and so on). These broad categories, however, had relatively little effect on behavior because they encompassed such a large proportion (over two-thirds) of state and local spending. As it turned out, these "official" designations of the uses of shared revenue, which were compiled and published annually by the Department of the Treasury in the early program years, were often highly political, and in the view of the General Accounting Office, "illusory."[6] For example, we found that many local officials regarded police protection as such a popular area of governmental activity that they reaped benefits by assigning revenue sharing dollars to public safety, often in cases in which our field researchers determined that the net effect of this infusion of federal aid funds was very different from what was officially reported.

We saw it as a chief part of our role to explain this fungibility phenomenon in describing the fiscal and programmatic effects of shared revenue. Over time, we developed increasingly better techniques for doing so. In our view, the official data from the Treasury on the uses of shared revenue, which were based on the broad spending categories mentioned earlier, were highly misleading. Shared revenue could be used for new purposes or to offset taxes, that is, for what public finance economists call substitution. If the funds were used for substitution purposes, other questions needed to be asked. In what types of jurisdictions was this likely to be the case and why? If shared revenue was used for new purposes, policymakers wanted to know what kinds of new purposes tended to benefit and why.

Despite the fact that our sample was a stratified and not a random sample, and despite the fact that we found it necessary to base our findings on field analyses that could not be replicated (or at least not easily or systematically replicated), we found that we were able to generalize in ways that could help policymakers come to grips with these and other issues about the effects of the revenue sharing program. In every case, we tried to be as clear as possible about our research method, its strengths and limitations. We saw our role as providing research data that would allow users (including many policymakers) to make *their own* decisions about the success or failure of this program, according to their views about the purposes of revenue sharing. As members of the research group, we had our own ideas about the aims and benefits of the revenue sharing program. Some of us participated in policy discussions on this basis. But all of us tried to make a distinction between what we had learned about the effects of the program and what we thought about them.

Sometimes the way the issues were framed surprised us. In the course of the debate on the first extension of revenue sharing legislation (altogether there were three extensions of the program), it became apparent that substitution uses of shared revenue were not always regarded as a bad outcome by politicians. Conservative members of Congress in some cases supported revenue sharing as a way to relieve the pressure on local property taxes. Likewise, some liberal politicians, concerned about the plight of distressed cities, saw this tax-relief effect as an important benefit, enabling these distressed cities to compete for business and residents on a better footing.

At the 1975 Senate hearings on the renewal of revenue sharing, Kenneth A. Gibson, mayor of Newark, New Jersey (one of the nation's most economically distressed cities with the highest effective property tax rate among large cities), testified on precisely this point. Gibson said that revenue sharing "enabled us to provide public services while, in fact, reducing an already overburdened property tax structure."[7] As it turned out, Newark was included as one of the jurisdictions in the Brookings evaluation study, and the point made by Gibson came up frequently in the discussion of our findings, often with Newark as an illustration. According to our field researcher for Newark, at the outset of revenue sharing, as Mayor Gibson had indicated, the city used its shared revenue to stabilize and reduce its property tax: "This is what city officials felt was most urgently needed to improve the relative economic position of the city and enhance its ability to hold and attract residential and business property owners."[8]

The Decision to Evaluate Revenue Sharing

American domestic policy is made in spurts. The spigot is opened widest in the early years of a new administration. Classic cases are Franklin Delano Roosevelt's New Deal and the outpouring of new social legislation following Lyndon Johnson's election in 1964. A similar spurt of new domestic laws came in the first term of the Nixon administration in the form of his New Federalism initiatives, especially revenue sharing and block grants.

It is now commonplace for observers of the Great Society period to view the results of Johnson's new social programs as having failed to deal with the nation's social ills. I believe that the role of social scientists in the Great Society period focused too much on policy formulation. Not enough attention was given to the evaluation of programs once they were adopted. As already stated, I was a participant in the spurt of domestic policymaking in Nixon's first term. When I returned to Brookings in 1974, I worked on the evaluation of these New Federalism programs. My attitude was that whether they succeeded, needed revision, fell apart, or worked badly, at least these conclusions would be reached through systematic, in-depth evaluation studies by social scientists.

Readers may ask how a participant in the policy process (presumably a person committed to what comes out) can evaluate the results. One response is obvious: social scientists should be as objective as possible in conducting evaluation research. Second, the Brookings-based field network evaluation studies involved many participants; a research manager would be hard put to insert a bias into the findings of the thirty or so social scientists who were part of these networks. I felt comfortable in the role of evaluating programs I had helped to design because of the way the social science research industry operates. Other evaluation studies of revenue sharing gave the users of this body of research an opportunity to compare and cross-check our results. In this way, the existence of multiple evaluation studies of those programs large enough and important enough to warrant such attention helps to keep the evaluation industry honest and aboveboard.

Highlights of the Findings

On the whole and over time we found that about half of the shared revenue received by the local governments in the sample for our study was used for new spending purposes and about half for various substitutive uses such as reducing or holding down taxes and maintaining programs that according to the field research would otherwise have been reduced or eliminated. For state governments in the sample, the proportion of shared revenue allocated to new purposes was lower, about one-third.

When the field researchers found a new spending effect of shared revenue, they were asked to present information about the types of new spending. We found (and this is intuitively logical) that the predominant new spending purposes were for capital items, often roads and road work on the part of smaller jurisdictions. The reasoning of local officials in concentrating shared revenue on capital expenditures in this way was that since they did not trust the federal government to stay its course they were reluctant to allocate shared revenue to operating purposes. If they did so, they feared they would get caught short when the federal government eliminated or reduced the revenue sharing program. They would then be faced with pressures to raise taxes to continue programs paid for out of revenue sharing. Substitutive uses of revenue sharing funds were found to be highest in fiscally distressed jurisdictions, for example, declining central cities. Table 8.1 summarizes the findings of the first two rounds of field research.

These determinations of the fiscal effects of revenue sharing were a necessary first step in studying the programmatic and decentralization effects of the revenue sharing program. If there was new spending, what programs benefited? Did revenue sharing give more prominence and importance to the

TABLE 8.1

Mean Percentages of Shared Revenue Allocated by Sample Jurisdictions, by Type of Net Fiscal Effect, Local and State

Net Fiscal Effect	Round 1	Round 2	Cumulative
Local governments[a]			
New spending	**56.2**	**45.9**	**51.8**
New capital	45.2	34.5	41.4
Expanded operations	10.5	10.6	9.6
Increased pay and benefits	0.5	0.8	0.8
Substitutions	**43.9**	**52.4**	**47.0**
Program maintenance	12.8	14.6	13.5
Restoration of federal aid	0.4	1.1	0.8
Tax reduction	3.8	5.0	4.4
Tax stabilization	14.1	18.3	15.3
Avoidance of borrowing	9.6	7.7	8.8
Increased fund balance	2.8	3.4	3.0
Substitution not categorized	0.4	2.3	1.2
Balance of allocation[b]	**0.1**	**1.6**	**1.2**
State governments			
New spending	**35.7**	**39.6**	**37.3**
New capital	21.1	21.0	21.0
Expanded operations	12.1	13.2	13.8
Increased pay and benefits	0.0	5.4	1.2
New spending not categorized	2.5	0.0	1.3
Substitutions	**64.3**	**58.2**	**62.5**
Program maintenance	15.3	0.0	6.7
Restoration of federal aid	3.0	13.3	7.8
Tax reduction	13.2	12.0	12.2
Tax stabilization	0.0	12.5	7.6
Avoidance of borrowing	3.3	2.5	4.0
Increased fund balance	4.5	5.4	4.6
Substitution not categorized	25.0	12.5	19.6
Balance of allocation[b]	**0.0**	**2.4**	**0.1**

Source: Richard P. Nathan, Charles F. Adams, Jr., et al., *Revenue Sharing: The Second Round* (Washington, D.C.: The Brookings Institution, 1977), p. 31.

Note: Figures may not add to totals because of rounding. It should also be noted that the cumulative figures do not coincide with a simple averaging of the first- and second-round figures because of differences within jurisdictions in the amounts allocated in the two rounds.

[a]In round 1, three local governments allocated no revenue sharing funds and, therefore, were not included in the first round summaries. In round 2, one local government made no allocation and was excluded from the second round summaries.
[b]Net effect not categorized as between new spending and substitution.

decision processes of governments "close to the people"? Did
it reduce federal controls and influence? What types of political actors were most affected? Institutional questions like these
reflect the decentralization purpose of revenue sharing that
Nixon and many of the program's Republican supporters particularly favored. We used a common conceptual framework to
understand these effects, asking the field researchers to identify
the key political actors in decisions about the uses of revenue
sharing funds by major type (generalist, specialist, elected, career) and to indicate the nature and degree of change (if any)
in their roles and relationships as a result of the receipt of
revenue sharing funds. One can summarize the data on the way
revenue sharing affected state and local political processes in
the following terms: while revenue sharing was found to have
enhanced the role of generalist officials vis-à-vis specialized
agencies and interest groups, its effects in these terms were not
highly visible or dramatic.

As implied in the foregoing discussion, I believe that a good
test of public policy research is whether the findings were
useful and used in the policy process. Was the research method
decided upon convincing and clear? There were, and still are,
marked differences in point of view among adherents of the
research methods mentioned in this chapter. Despite these
debates within the research fraternity, members in good standing are able to apply generally agreed-upon standards for the
scientific integrity of the execution of the methods used in a
given public policy research project. The bubbling cauldron of
the review and comment procedures in public policy research
gives signals to politicians which, without being highly explicit,
determine the application and value of social science knowledge in the governmental process. This is not to say that the
review process always works well and that mistakes are never
made, but it does permit different kinds of styles of social

science knowledge to flow into the governmental process. The field network evaluation methodology has its strengths and weaknesses, friends and detractors. The test of whether findings were useful and used in policymaking is not a highly sensitive indicator of quality or consensus among social scientists, but it does work reasonably well.

While the Brookings-based revenue sharing study was under way, Congress enacted two of Nixon's proposed block grants, one for community development and one for employment and training programs. In both cases, the researchers in the Brookings field evaluation network that conducted the revenue sharing study were asked by government agencies to conduct a field evaluation study of these programs. With modifications to reflect the learning experience and the different characteristics of the programs being evaluated, the research methodology used in these other studies was similar to that described in this chapter for the revenue sharing program. In one study, of the large and controversial public service employment program under the Comprehensive Employment and Training Act (CETA), the "complementarity approach" described in this chapter was also used to compare the results of the field research with those of a parallel statistical analysis using econometric methods to estimate the job creation versus displacement effects of the public service jobs program. Actually, the employment and training field is one of the busiest byways of evaluation research in the field of domestic public affairs, no doubt because of the active interest of labor economists in these types of studies. The field network evaluation study and related studies of public service employment programs is the subject of the next chapter.

9

Employment and Training
Evaluation Research

ONE OF the main ideas in this set of chapters on evaluation research is the need to take a systems approach to public policy research. The field of employment and training research, taken as a whole, offers a good vantage point for considering the idea of a systems approach to public policy research because there is such a cornucopia of material. Labor economists have played an especially strong role in the design and conduct of evaluation studies. In this chapter, I consider further illustrations of evaluation research in the field of employment policy, both good practices and bad, as grist for thinking about changes in the approach to and organization of evaluation research. I begin this discussion with the study that I know best, the study conducted by the field network evaluation group initially based at the Brookings Institution, and modeled closely on the revenue sharing study described in chapter 8. This study of the public service employment program under the Comprehensive Employment and Training Act (CETA), initiated in June 1977, opened up some lively controversies about research methods for evaluating different kinds of program impacts.

The CETA Jobs Program

The Comprehensive Employment and Training Act was originally enacted in December 1973 in the form of a block grant as part of the Nixon administration's New Federalism program. Its purpose was to consolidate federal grants in this functional area to give greater discretion to state and local governments. Initially, most of the funds were for job training. Republicans resisted the idea of providing funds for the creation of new jobs, although many Democrats supported this. A public service employment program, which is a job-creation program, was authorized as a title of the original CETA law, but it was funded at a very low level. Later, the public service employment program was expanded substantially in order to combat the 1974–75 recession, despite resistance from the Ford administration. The public service jobs component of CETA was further revised and the level of spending was increased three times after 1974—in 1976, 1977, and 1978. This job-creation program continued in effect until 1981 when it was eliminated in the first year of the Reagan administration as part of the package of domestic budget cuts enacted in that year. (Reagan later replaced the training portion of the CETA law with a new block grant, mainly distributed to the states, called the Job Training Partnership Act, or JTPA.)

At its peak in April 1978, the CETA public service employment program employed 755,000 people at an annual spending rate of $7 billion. This made it by far the largest federal program in the employment and training field and in fact one of the largest federal grant-in-aid programs to states and localities. (It was, however, considerably smaller than the Works Progress Administration [WPA] of the Depression years, which at its peak employed 3 million people.) This expanded version of the CETA public service employment program was an obvious target for Reagan-era budget cutters in the retrenchment mood of the 1980s, if for no other reason than simply because it was so big. Its vulnerability was compounded by the program's reputation for waste and abuses. The CETA job-creation program, in short, had few friends and lots of enemies in 1981 when Reagan came into office.

As in the case of the revenue sharing program, the CETA job-creation program had several purposes; in the usual workings of the American political system, these goals were not clearly stated or weighted. The three main objectives were to provide jobs for the unemployed in recession periods; to aid disadvantaged persons in developing skills and obtaining job experience; and to assist state and local governments in providing needed public services.

In 1976, when the CETA public service employment program was revised for the second time, Senator Henry L. Bellmon (R-Okla.) added an amendment to address an issue that was then a source of lively controversy, the concern that public service jobs were being used by state and local governments to displace workers who otherwise would have been on the state or city payroll. Some opponents of the public service jobs program charged that it was simply a hidden subsidy to state and local governments and that it did not increase employment or provide additional public services. Bellmon's amendment directed the National Commission for Employment Policy (a permanent research and advisory group chartered under federal law) to make a study of the "net employment effects" of the public service employment program. In turn, the commission, chaired by Eli Ginzberg, contracted with the Brookings Institution to have this research conducted by the field evaluation research group using the methodology described in chapter 8 for the study of the revenue sharing program. (The Brookings field network evaluation group in the meantime had conducted a study, similar to the revenue sharing study, of the community development block grant, the other major block grant program enacted as part of Nixon's New Federalism agenda.)[1] The field evaluation study of the CETA public service jobs program was started at the Brookings Institution and was completed at the Woodrow Wilson School, Princeton University.

The choice of the field evaluation approach to conduct this research is an interesting one. Before 1976, there had been a number of smaller-scale and more theoretical studies conducted by labor economists of the intergovernmental displacement issue under public service employment programs. This research was in the form of statistical studies using econometric techniques and available program and demographic data. A preliminary paper written by labor economist George Johnson for the Department of Labor reached the conclusion that the job-displacement impact of a federally funded public service employment program would be very large.[2] Although these findings were labeled as tentative, considerable attention was given to Johnson's main conclusion that in the long run the displacement effect of grants-in-aid provided for public service job creation would absorb all, or nearly all, of the funds appropriated for this purpose. Johnson's econometric approach is not the only way to answer this hard question about the job-displacement effects of public service employment grants to state and local governments. By contracting with the Brookings-based field network to conduct the study mandated under the Bellmon amendment, the National Commission for Employment Policy was bringing an alternative methodology to bear on this issue. Researchers, as noted earlier, refer to this strategy as "triangulation," conducting multiple studies using different methods to see if the findings converge.

The Field Evaluation

It was in this setting that the Brookings-based field network turned its attention in 1976 to a longitudinal evaluation of the effects of the CETA public service employment program. A group of thirty field researchers (as in the past, approximately equally divided between economists and political scientists) conducted four rounds of field observations in forty state and local governments. The sample included three types of CETA program sponsors: (1) large local units (over 100,000 population) that qualified as "local prime sponsors" under CETA; (2) consortia of local units designated as "local prime sponsors"; and (3) state governments responsible for administering CETA programs in the "balance of state" areas. Within these jurisdictions, funds for job creation were channeled to thousands of public and nonprofit agencies, thus greatly expanding the screen for the field analysis and requiring a sampling procedure for selecting the organizations for detailed analysis. Because a number of large jurisdictions were included in the sample, the study sites accounted for 10 percent of all enrollees in the CETA public service employment program.

As in the previous field network evaluation studies, the research design included a number of categories of effects that enabled the researchers to study this program on a broad basis. The study was not limited to the job-displacement issue. It also dealt with questions involving the fiscal impact of CETA job funds; the types of jobs provided; the public services affected; the agencies that administered the program and their implementation processes; the training provided to participants; and the effect of CETA jobs funds on nonprofit organizations. The research approach and analytical framework were developed through consultations with the central staff and the field researchers.

As it turned out, the bottom-line finding of the Brookings-Princeton study on the job-displacement issue was very different from that of the earlier analysis conducted by George Johnson.[3] His paper had indicated a very high (eventually total) job-displacement effect for the CETA public service employment program. By contrast, we found what many observers regarded as a surprisingly low level of job displacement. For the sample as a whole, approximately one-fifth of the positions studied were assigned by the field researchers (in consultation with the study's central staff) to job displacement. These findings were issued in a series of reports published by the National Commission for Employment Policy and were later summarized in a Brookings book and related papers and articles. These publications carefully described the research methodology and provided illustrations, drawing on statements in the reports submitted by the field researchers, of the kinds of determinations that were made in assigning the positions studied to the various employment-effect categories used by the field researchers.

A number of reasons appeared to explain why local officials (most of these funds went to local governments) were reluctant to use CETA public service employment funds for displacement purposes. One reason, and it is a reason that experts in the field have not taken seriously enough, is that the law prohibited displacement. A second reason for the relatively low level of displacement is that local officials in many cases shared the national objective of creating jobs to relieve unemployment.

However, in even more basic terms, the field researchers reported that officials in the study sites were reluctant to use CETA job-creation funds for displacement because of the possible long-term consequences. These local officials had been "burned" by federal policy changes. In the case of the CETA public employment program, there was a particularly high level of uncertainty about the future intentions of the federal government. A major concern on the part of local officials, also found in the case of the revenue sharing program, was that when this federal largesse was ended, or if the rules for its use were changed (both events later occurred), they would be left holding the bag. They would face strong political pressures to increase taxes in order to continue to pay their regular employees, who were being supported with CETA funds, if they had used these funds for job displacement. This was a risk that local officials simply did not want to take. There was one exception. In jurisdictions facing heavy fiscal pressure (mainly distressed central cities), displacement tended to be higher under the CETA job program than in other jurisdictions, attributable, according to our interpretation, to the need (or at least the perceived need) to use every available dollar to maintain basic services.

Another important and related finding was the fact that many of these positions were not filled by local governments or other public authorities, but were instead suballocated to nonprofit organizations. An increasing percentage of these positions were contracted out to nonprofit, mostly community-based, organizations that offered social and community development services. In the first round of the field research, one-quarter of the positions accounted for by the sample were subcontracted to nonprofit organizations; by the second round of the field research, this ratio had risen to nearly one-half.[4]

Our reports of relatively low-level displacement were widely noted both in the political and academic arenas because they were contrary to what many (including some of the researchers in the field network) had expected. These findings stirred controversy. Two meetings in particular stand out in my memory. The first was with Senator Bellmon. I was told by the staff of the National Commission for Employment Policy that he had read our first report, which was issued in March 1978, and that he wanted to talk to me about it. I was apprehensive since Bellmon had previously indicated his opinion that CETA job-creation funds were highly substitutive. At our meeting Senator Bellmon said that although he had been skeptical about our results when he first learned about them, after reading our report he was convinced by our conclusions and explanations about our findings.

The second memorable meeting at which the results of this research were discussed was arranged by the staff of the National Commission for Employment Policy to discuss the two main approaches used to analyze the net employment effects of the CETA public service employment program, the field evaluation approach and the econometric approach. George Johnson and I were the principal speakers. The audience was relatively large for a meeting in Washington on research methodology (about sixty people); it included both researchers and experts in the field of employment and training. This meeting, true to the academic style, involved an intense discussion (really a debate) about the validity of the competing research approaches. I recall that those of us working on the field network evaluation study came away from this confrontation with a good feeling about the reactions to our presentation. The fact that this second meeting was so spirited shows that the paradigms and methods of applied social science often can be topics of intense feelings.

The Complementarity Approach

As stressed in chapter 8, a major premise of the work of the field evaluation research group is that the distinction between the field evaluation and econometric methods is not an either/ or proposition. In two of the studies, of revenue sharing and

CETA public service jobs, members of the field research group conducted what we referred to as "complementary" statistical studies of the intergovernmental impact of the grant-in-aid program. In the case of the CETA public service employment program, the results of this complementary statistical analysis, using a pooled time-series approach, were published in the *Journal of Human Resources* and subjected to the hard scrutiny of academic peer review.[5]

The basic idea of this complementary approach is to use insights from the field research to build "a better mousetrap" for lessons and doing a statistical analysis. For example, the high degree of subcontracting to nonprofit organizations under the CETA job-creation program turned out to make a substantial difference in our statistical research. The first step in conducting the statistical analysis was to review the earlier econometric studies. We found that the failure to take into account the kinds of on-the-scene lessons learned in the field research, in this case the importance of the subcontracting of CETA public service jobs, caused considerable distortion. In the early econometric studies, it was assumed that all of the CETA job-creation funds allocated to a given jurisdiction were paid as wages by that government. If instead some of these funds were subcontracted to nonprofit organizations, or if they were suballocated to other public entities, as was often the case for local school districts, this could have the effect of creating what appeared to be (but was not) a job-displacement effect in a purely statistical analysis.[6]

Another aspect of the field research of consequence in the complementary statistical analysis involved the timing of the receipt and use of CETA job funds. Centrally available data (mostly from the Census of Governments conducted by the Bureau of the Census) did not fit well with the receipt-and-spending cycle for CETA job funds. It was necessary to adjust for timing differences in the statistical analysis. In our statistical study we did this by using unpublished worksheets from the Bureau of the Census that showed the actual receipt-and-spending cycle for CETA funds for the thirty municipal governments included in our statistical analysis. (The thirty cities were large jurisdictions for which detailed data on CETA grant funds were available from the Census Bureau.)

The results of the complementary statistical analysis informed by the field research were very similar to those found in the field evaluation study. In both cases, the methodology was spelled out carefully and both the methodology and findings were related to other studies in the field.

Studies of Individual Impacts under CETA

So far this chapter has described the employment effects of the CETA public service job program on the recipient jurisdictions. Our study also dealt with the effects of the CETA jobs program on the finances, programs, and management processes of the recipient jurisdictions.[7] These effects on jurisdictions were not the foremost concern of researchers and policymakers, however. The dominant concern was the impact of CETA programs on *individuals.* In this research arena more than any other, evaluation research for large, ongoing service-type programs shows that individual impact research is fraught with logistical, political, and scientific problems.

Several characteristics of CETA programs (both the training and the job-creation programs) produced problems for research on effects on individuals. One is the "federalism barrier reef." The CETA programs were administered on a decentralized basis by state and local governments; this involved thousands of localities and hundreds of thousands of local public agencies and nonprofit organizations. The data comparability problems inherent in such a program structure should give any self-respecting econometrician pause. But that is not all.

A second problem for individual impact research was that CETA programs were so widespread, visible to the eligible groups, and often controversial that the real politics of local public jobs programs at the time discouraged the use of an evaluation research design based on the random assignment of some persons to an untreated control group. It would have been extremely hard for even the most supportive CETA program managers to arrange to have a randomly selected, untreated control group under these conditions. As is brought out in the sections that follow, none of the evaluation studies of the impacts of CETA programs on individuals used a research design with random assignment.

A third obstacle to evaluation research on the impacts on individuals of CETA programs is what might be called the "marginality problem." This is related to the earlier discussion of the null hypothesis. The typical CETA intervention was not that long or large. There is reason to question whether such programs and services by themselves could have been expected to have a discernible and lasting impact on the lives of the participants, considering the great number of forces and factors (both public and private) that influence the way human beings develop and change in a complex, technologically advanced society.

I served on the advisory committee for a large survey research project on the impact of CETA programs funded by the Department of Labor, called the Continuous Longitudinal Manpower Survey (CLMS), begun in 1974. To facilitate the CLMS data-collection system, the Labor Department contracted with the Bureau of the Census to have the bureau survey a succession of cohort groups entering various components of the CETA program. Altogether, more than 6,000 people participated in this study; there was a baseline interview and in most cases four follow-up surveys for the people in this sample.

But, even after interviewing all the CETA participants, one faced the perennial question, *compared to what?* Observations about the experience of participants during and after the CETA programs would not reveal the extent to which the programs did or did not assist them. There is value, of course, in knowing what CETA services were provided and what types of people received them. But it is reasonable to ask whether an investment as large as that for the CLMS should have been undertaken if this was its only output.

The advisory committee wrestled with this issue about establishing the counterfactual state, as did the staff of the Labor Department and the researchers with whom the department contracted. (Westat, Inc., of Rockville, Maryland, conducted most of the analysis for this study.) The solution decided upon was to rely heavily on data from an existing file, the Current Population Survey conducted by the Census Bureau, which in March of each year includes an enlarged sample and a special survey instrument on the employment experience of respondents. These data, however, are cross-sectional. They are collected at one point in time. Respondents are not reinterviewed as is done in the collection of longitudinal data. To overcome this problem, data from the Current Population Survey were linked with the earnings records of people in the sample obtained from the Social Security Administration on a confidential basis (that is, individual respondents could not be identified). In this way, a "matched file" was constructed with characteristics similar to those of the people in the CETA programs.

Labor Department technical reports on this research were candid in discussing the drawbacks of this approach for establishing a comparison group. Contamination was one problem. There was no way of knowing whether the people in the "matched file" received CETA or similar employment and training services. Furthermore, there was evidence that the Social Security earnings records (critical to the analysis because earned income after the CETA program was the key dependent variable) did not include some types of earnings. For example, wage and salary payments to state and local government employees were not at this time included in Social Security files.

One of the early reports on the CLMS contains this depressing statement: "One simply cannot say at this time how comparable the comparison groups are to the participant groups in the absence of the CETA program."[8] The Labor Department continued to try to work out the wrinkles, and progress was made. Nevertheless, a report issued two years later on this study contains a caveat very similar to that just quoted: "As in all program evaluations where it is not feasible to randomly assign potential participants to the program or to a control group, there is some uncertainty about the amount of selectivity bias in the estimates of net impact."[9]

Other experts in the field were not so restrained in their comments; the small tempest among experts about whether the CLMS was worth the price continued. When the Reagan administration won enactment of the successor program to CETA (the Job Training Partnership Act) in 1982, the controversy heated up again. An elaborate data-collection system like the CLMS was established as the basis for research on the impact of the JTPA program. In the end, it was decided not to use these data for research on JTPA. The survey was eventually discontinued. Instead, the U.S. Department of Labor decided to conduct studies with random assignment to ascertain the impact on individuals of JTPA services. The Manpower Demonstration Research Corporation is one of the organizations involved in this research. As of 1988, there are three ongoing evaluation studies in the field of human resource programs that use a research design grounded in random assignment to assess the impact of a large ongoing program on individual participants. They are the JTPA study, a similar food stamp employment and training study, and the California GAIN evaluation research.

Several of our themes—emphasizing the challenge of evaluation research, taking the institutional dimension into account, the problem in such studies of measuring individual impacts, and adopting a combined systems approach to demonstration and evaluation research—all come into play in the field of employment and training. The story is still unfolding. What should be done to improve our capacity to conduct demonstration and evaluation research is becoming clearer, but that does not mean we know everything necessary about how to proceed. The management tasks involved in identifying, recruiting, and organizing the researchers who conduct both demonstration and evaluation public policy research are the subject of the final chapter.

IO

Lessons and Implications

THE ROLE of the sponsors and funders of applied social science research is critical if we are to succeed in strengthening the linkages between social science and social policy.

Sponsors of Policy Research

Two main types of institutions in the United States sponsor applied social science research as an input to domestic policy-making and its execution—government agencies and private foundations. The rise and fall of applied social science in domestic policy in the postwar period is primarily a reflection of the activities of the U.S. government. Since World War II, the federal government has played the dominant role in providing funds for this purpose. A survey of federal government agencies by the National Academy of Sciences identified $1.8 billion in social "knowledge production and application" activities in 1976.[1] The survey showed that this spending represented a tripling of the commitment of federal funds to these activities since the early 1960s. Unfortunately, we do not have comparable data for the intervening years or the period since 1976. As it happens, however, 1976 probably was the peak year (or close to it) of government support for applied social science in the postwar period in the United States. Most of the federal funds devoted to social knowledge production and application, according to the survey by the National Academy of Sciences, was spent by a few agencies. The Department of Health, Education, and Welfare headed the list, accounting for $729 million in 1976.

Private foundations are another major source of funds for applied social science research. In the 1970s, the government's role overshadowed that of foundations. But as government pulled back from applied social science research in the 1980s, the contribution of foundations has become more important, although, again, we do not have comparable data to those presented in the National Academy of Sciences study to show this relationship.

In both government and foundations, grant officers play the key role in decisions about the types of applied social science research to be supported. Their usual mode of operation is to recommend that particular grants be made to outside researchers, although in some cases they decide what studies should be undertaken by researchers within the government agency or the foundation by which they are employed.

Grant officers are responsible for bringing together money and social science researchers in the conduct of public policy research. It is this vantage point, the role of grant officers, that is highlighted in this chapter: how can they advance the themes presented in this book?

An abbreviation that lights up telephone switchboards in research centers across the land is "RFP," request for proposals. This is the most common research-contracting process in government whereby grant officers develop a statement of their research objectives and invite bidders to respond to them. The use of RFPs is appropriate for government. Public agencies should not play favorites. As the sponsors of social science research, they should give all research organizations a chance to participate. In practice, however, this is not always the way it works. Different administrations in Washington have been known to choose research proposals that fit their preferences of style and methodology or their ideological proclivities. The Carter and Reagan administrations often used an ostensibly open and competitive bidding system but ultimately selected the research organizations that reflected their own ideological orientations and preferences.

The RFP system is not the only way government agencies organize sponsored research. In some instances, they justify a sole-source procedure to select researchers for a project on the grounds that the need is urgent and only one organization has the background, capability, and experience to perform the necessary tasks on the schedule required by the contracting agency. Another approach is to invite a selected group of bidders from a roster of qualified research organizations to make proposals.

Policy research sponsored by foundations tends to be organized on a less formal basis than research sponsored by public agencies. Grant officers in foundations may use all three of the approaches just described, but the sole-source or invited-bidders approaches are most common.

Expert advisors also play a significant role in the conduct of applied social science research. These outside consultants help to develop research plans, review proposals, and monitor the progress of policy studies. Typically, they are senior professionals who for one reason or another do not choose to participate in a particular study.

Another crucial set of actors includes the leaders of the three main types of organizations that conduct policy research— university research centers, nonprofit research centers, and profit-making firms—who often have their own ideas about the conduct of applied social science research and their own contacts and resources. They are not always predisposed to fulfill the objectives advocated in this book. Persuading these leaders to work across disciplines, to adopt particular research designs and methods, and to integrate their activities with those of other research organizations requires substantial managerial and diplomatic skill on the part of grant officers. Not only must grant officers make the right choices of researchers and research organizations at the outset of a study, they must also effectively oversee the study to make certain that both the letter and spirit of the plans and agreements are followed.

Constituencies of Grant Officers

Grant officers have two main constituencies that they are likely to want (or need) to satisfy. The first group is the higher-level officials who must approve their decisions. In this respect, government agencies and private foundations differ. Within government, grant officers must satisfy the dominant political leadership group; for example, they must take cognizance of (and in some cases adhere to) the ideological and policy preferences of a liberal Great Society or a conservative Reaganite administration. Grant officers also must please programmatic officials (that is, program managers) who administer certain types of activity or specific government programs. To complicate matters, the interests of these two groups of agency officials often conflict.

Grant officers in foundations generally face a less complicated political setting. Their recommendations are reviewed (often perfunctorily) by a board of directors. In large foundations, higher-level officials often must also approve their decisions.

The second major constituency of grant officers both in government and in foundations is one that often means more to them. I refer to *science,* specifically the scientific discipline of a grant officer. In many situations the officer's scientific background substantially influences the type of public policy research that is undertaken. Throughout this book I have stressed the dominance of the intellectual paradigm, research methods, and interests of economists in public policy research since the mid-1960s. If a grant officer is trained as an economist, as is often the case, this is likely to be a telling factor, consciously or unconsciously, in decisions about the nature and purposes of public policy research projects.

The critical point here is that foundations and government agencies, and more specifically grant officers, are the politicians of policy research. They are the agents of change who can move in the directions urged in this book. The next two sections deal with the kinds of changes I believe would make a difference in the conduct of public policy research. They are organized according to the two types of public policy research highlighted in this volume, demonstration and evaluation research. Before proceeding, it is useful to restate my main themes:

1. Applied social science research in government should investigate *how to do things* more than what should be done. From my perspective, this means priority should be assigned to the two types of applied social science research considered in this book, *demonstration* studies to test new ideas and *evaluation* studies to assess ongoing programs. These two types of applied social science research should be favored over problem-identification studies of conditions and trends.

2. Demonstration and evaluation studies *differ* in ways that have not been sufficiently appreciated by the sponsors of public policy research and by researchers.

3. Public policy research should serve as a *two-way street*. The conduct of applied social science is not just a matter of what social science can do for the real world; it is also and very much a matter of what the real world can do for social science.

4. In designing and conducting public policy research, greater attention should be given to what I have referred to as the *missing links* of applied social science research *between disciplines within the social sciences* and those *between quantitative and qualitative* research methods and data.

5. In selecting the subjects for major demonstration and evaluation studies, priority should be given to situations in which three conditions apply: (a) policymakers are genuinely interested in the questions asked; (b) they are uncertain about the answers; and (c) they are willing to wait for answers.

Demonstration Research

Random assignment is the best starting point in summarizing what has been said about demonstration research. Social experimentation with random assignment is unique to the United States. As far as I can determine, no other Western countries have conducted social demonstration research with randomly assigned treatment and control groups. In the United States, two decades of experience with this form of policy research allows us now to take a hard look at its conduct and usefulness in the governmental process.

There is a consensus (actually almost a new orthodoxy) among both the funders of public policy research and the researchers in the United States that random assignment should be the strongly preferred approach to applied social science research to test new policies and programs. The reasoning is appealing. The more certain and definitive we can be in proving that something works, the better will be the position to argue in the political process that the tested treatment should be replicated.

We have seen, furthermore, that the sponsors of public policy research often test interventions they favor. They want to show that an idea that they approve of is likely to work and, if so, under what conditions and for what groups. This means that there is even more reason for grant officers to support studies using random assignment of participants to control and treatment groups, because this method helps to give credibility to the results of such studies. Random assignment provides political insulation for the sponsors of public policy research and for the social scientists who conduct it.

I have also argued that the case for demonstration research applies most strongly to service-type, rather than income-maintenance, programs. Government programs that redistribute income (either cash or in kind) typically apply to all who qualify for benefits. When such a universal policy is adopted, it is bound to be well and widely known. Hence, the public perception of the relationship between the state and the eligible population may shift because of the attention given to the debate about the adoption, for example, of what is described as a "guaranteed income" scheme. No amount of ingenuity in the design and conduct of demonstration research can control for the impact of such an attitude change. The same point applies to the consumption of medical and hospital services due to the changed environment in which the government has adopted a national health insurance program that is perceived as providing free or low-cost medical services to all who need them. Findings from research in an earlier (preprogram) period about the effects of a national health insurance scheme on the consumption of medical-care services may not hold up in a world in which such a program has actually been adopted.

On the other hand, such service-type interventions as supported work do not present this problem because they tend to be implemented selectively. Such programs operate in a limited geographical area or they concentrate on providing the service that is being tested to a relatively limited group that is believed to need it or to be likely to benefit most from a particular program. Moreover, service-type programs do not usually have the visibility and publicity that could in and of themselves change the expectations and behavior of large numbers of people.

In sum, I agree with the widespread view among policy researchers that random assignment should be the preferred methodology for applied social science research to test new programs, and I have a preference for focusing such studies on service-type interventions. These generalizations, however, do not end the matter. It is also necessary to consider the setting and practice of demonstration research.

Again, random assignment is our best starting point. In some situations demonstration research is a good idea and yet it is not desirable—perhaps even impossible—to use random assignment. I believe that grant officers in these circumstances should encourage research approaches that use program data or the findings from other demonstration studies as "benchmarks" for demonstration studies. This is bound to be easier and less expensive than conducting a whole new study with random assignment. In policy areas in which there is a sufficient body of experience with demonstration research based on random assignment, as in the field of employment and training programs for disadvantaged persons, we should be able to agree on benchmarks of program success from prior studies. Researchers could then measure the experience of the treatment group and compare it to these benchmarks.

There are also situations in which comparison groups, comparison sites, and econometric techniques (to model the counterfactual state statistically) are the appropriate approaches for demonstration studies. In some cases budget and political factors influence the decision to adopt one of these alternative approaches. In others, the small size of the program or of the population served or the loosely defined character of the treatment to be tested may preclude devoting the necessary resources to a demonstration study large enough and of long enough duration to warrant using random selection.

Another set of issues about demonstration research concerns *how* random assignment should be used. Demonstration studies with random assignment are expensive both in terms of monetary cost and in terms of the cost of having qualified social scientists devote the necessary time and energy to conducting them. I believe that when grant officers care enough to use the very best (that is, random assignment), demonstration studies should be conducted on a basis that maximizes what we learn. Most important of all, this requires combining social science disciplines; when we leave out disciplines in demonstration research, we leave out variables that from scientific and political standpoints could be vital to our understanding. This point is especially significant for two types of dependent variables, the *institutional* effects of the tested program and the *attitudes* of both providers and recipients of potential new public programs. We must avoid the fallacy of decomposition, by which I mean separating out economics, politics, and psychological variables in public policy research, a fallacy that unfortunately is endemic to modern social science.

According to this analysis, the two disciplines that need to be integrated more fully into public policy research are political science and psychology. Both involve methodologies that are not as systematic, cohesive, or widely accepted as those in economics. Political scientists tend to work in their own area or with their own style of inquiry without much genuine interchange or a shared corpus of theory. The situation is similar for psychologists. Realistically, achieving the kinds of linkages advocated in this book requires drawing upon subspecialities within the two disciplines. In the case of political science, researchers interested in studies of institutional behavior (especially the "new institutionalism" described in chapter 6) are obvious candidates for collaboration in demonstration research. Among psychologists, social psychologists are likely to be the best candidates as collaborators in multidisciplinary demonstration studies.

This need for linkages between social science disciplines is closely related to the second missing link discussed in this book—that between quantitative and qualitative research methods in applied social science research. Again, we have to consider the different approaches taken by economists, political scientists, and psychologists. The latter two disciplines rely much more heavily than do economists on qualitative research methods and data. The challenge for grant officers is to bring the best practices of both fields into genuine partnership relationships with economists in the conduct of demonstration research. At its roots, this requires the encouragement of more flexible and generally less rigorous approaches to demonstration studies on a basis that reflects the complexity of the real world and the limits of social science.

One final point is related to the desirability of broader and more flexible approaches to the conduct of demonstration research. As discussed in chapter 4, I believe that demonstration research should concentrate on measured impacts. I am uneasy about cost-benefit analyses that purport to be all-encompassing and that extrapolate the long-term costs and benefits of the treatment being tested. This is not to say we should ignore costs in assessing the results of demonstration studies or that we should be unwilling to consider the longer-term effects of a program tested in a demonstration study. My concern is with the presumably comprehensive approach of many cost-benefit analyses. Such analyses often make far-reaching assumptions about the future impacts of both measured and unmeasured program effects. In this way, they can give a mistaken (or at least exaggerated) impression that the results of this final step in the research process are the definitive bottom-line findings of a demonstration study. We need to be very careful about this.

Evaluation Research

The differences between demonstration and evaluation studies must be recognized by the sponsors and practitioners of applied social science research. Again, random assignment is one of the keys to this difference. There is a role for random assignment under some conditions in evaluation research, but it is often a smaller and less critical role than in the case of demonstration research. Once a new program is launched, the terrain is harder to deal with in a way that enables us to make precise statements about the nature of the treatment and arrange to withhold these services in specific locales or from some people for research purposes.

It is not only the scientific terrain that becomes more difficult when the question for policy research shifts from testing possible new programs to assessing the effects of ongoing programs. Politicians often ask questions about existing programs that differ from their questions about the potential new programs tested in a demonstration study. Demonstration research helps politicians to decide what to do. Once they have decided to adopt a new program, *institutional* issues often take on a much higher priority: do the institutions and organizations that are supposed to implement a given policy do so in the way that was intended?

Earlier, I used the example of a grant-in-aid program for

computer-assisted reading remediation to illustrate this point. Under such a program, if policymakers can change the behavior of school systems and educational administrators, they may believe (and with good reason) that this will ultimately increase the reading proficiency of individual students. A similar point was made in the case of revenue sharing where a major aim was to decentralize governmental decision making. In such situations, politicians may be most interested, or exclusively interested, in studying the institutional effects of a new program instead of its impacts on individual citizens. One reason for this is what I have called the "federalism barrier reef," which must be taken into account by the sponsors, planners, and practitioners of public policy research.

The questions we ask about institutional behavior are not entirely different from those we ask in demonstration studies. We are still interested in the *counterfactual state.* Did institutional behavior change in ways that are different from what would have been the case in the absence of the program we are studying? The catch, and it is a serious shortcoming, is that we are not in as good a position to use random assignment and the statistical inference procedures that this unleashes to measure these institutional effects.

Implicit in this discussion is the political perspective of officials above the agency level, for example, members of Congress or cabinet officials. In the case of evaluation research government grant officers must also deal with another important constituency group, the program officials of their agency. It is not unusual for these officials who administer the program being studied to view evaluation research as a threat. As we have seen, evaluation studies focused on impacts on individual recipients often produce findings that are far short of the kinds of claims (often exaggerated) made in the political process in jockeying for authority and funds for one's cherished program. Hence, agency officials are likely to be more comfortable asking questions about institutional effects (What happened to the political system?) as opposed to the question highlighted in demonstration research (What worked?). Feedback from an implementation study is more easily accommodated in the political process. If a program I favor as an agency official is not implemented according to plan, I can change my plan much more easily than if my research staff tells me (and is likely to tell the world around me) that my program does not work, that it does not produce the results we intended and claimed for it.

Even when we do seek to analyze the individual impacts of existing programs in evaluation research, the necessary first step is implementation research to lay the groundwork for a rigorous and structured study of a program's impacts on individual recipients or participants. Once we understand the landscape in these terms, research focused on individuals, perhaps based on random assignment, may be justified, but this second step is not always desirable, and in some cases it is not possible. These two steps in evaluation research—implementation research and individual impact research—were highlighted in the discussion of the *systems approach* to evaluation research.

A Modest Proposal

An important purpose of this chapter is to urge that more attention be given to the politics and management of applied social science research. I have urged that social scientists from disciplines other than economics should be made full partners in demonstration and evaluation studies. This section advances a modest proposal in this direction.

Even where the responsible agencies or foundation grant officers and advisors are committed to making changes in the organization and conduct of public policy research, we need to consider how we can obtain cooperation from the best qualified social science researchers to participate in innovative, and perhaps risky, demonstration and evaluation studies on a multidisciplinary basis. For this purpose, I recommend "follow-up grants," grants to researchers who participate in multidisciplinary applied social science research projects. The idea of follow-up grants is simple; they would enable researchers who participate in multidisciplinary applied studies to use the resulting data for their own scholarly work once the research (or their part of the research) is completed. Specifically, such grants would permit the participating scholars to devote a certain amount of time (for example, one year, a summer, or a semester) after their involvement in a major demonstration or evaluation study to mine the data set they helped to produce to publish papers and articles in their own field. Such grants would have a double social utility. They would enhance our ability to benefit from the participation of leading scholars in multidisciplinary studies; at the same time they would help to make applied social science research a two-way street, contributing to both public policy and social science scholarship.

More than anything else the ideas advocated here require a conviction on the part of the sponsors of public policy research that success in pursuing strategies to promote multidisciplinary demonstration and evaluation studies will ultimately improve the practice and increase the value of applied social science in government policymaking. The challenge of obtaining resources and changing the behavior of researchers and research organizations is formidable. One is reminded of a saying by Einstein: "I have little patience with scientists who take a board of wood, look for its thinnest part, and drill a great number of holes where the drilling is easy."[2] Changing the agenda and approach of applied social science research as an input to the governmental process is worthwhile despite the difficulties.

NOTES

Chapter 1

1. Robert A. Scott and Arnold R. Shore, *Why Sociology Does Not Apply: A Study of the Use of Sociology in Public Policy* (New York: Elsevier, 1979).

2. Henry J. Aaron, *Politics and the Professors: The Great Society in Perspective* (Washington, D.C.: The Brookings Institution, 1978).

3. Charles Murray, *Losing Ground: American Social Policy, 1950–1980* (New York: Basic Books, 1984), p. 36.

4. Jonathan Swift, *Gulliver's Travels* (New York: Dell, 1961), pp. 210, 214–15.

5. Karen Davis, "Research and Policy Formulation," in *Applications of Social Science to Clinical Medicine and Health Policy*, Linda H. Aiken and David Mechanic, eds. (New Brunswick, N.J.: Rutgers University Press, 1986), p. 122.

6. Aaron Wildavsky, *Speaking Truth to Power* (Boston: Little, Brown, 1979), pp. 13, 19.

7. Beatrice Webb, *My Apprenticeship* (Cambridge: Cambridge University Press, 1979), pp. 139–40.

8. Joseph Schumpeter, *Capitalism, Socialism, and Democracy* (London: George Allen and Unwin, 1976), p. 45.

9. Abraham Kaplan, *The Conduct of Inquiry: Methodology for Behavioral Science* (Scranton, Penn.: Chandler, 1964), p. 39.

10. Ibid., p. 26.

11. Daniel Patrick Moynihan, *Maximum Feasible Misunderstanding: Community Action in the War on Poverty* (New York: Free Press, 1969), p. 193.

12. Mary Jo Bane and David T. Ellwood, "The Dynamics of Dependence: The Routes to Self-Sufficiency," Urban Systems Research and Engineering, Cambridge, Mass., June 1983, prepared for the U.S. Department of Health and Human Services, p. 11. A paper by Charles Murray that also uses the PSID data dramatizes the kinds of differences that have emerged in interpretations of these data. His conclusions are very different from those of Greg J. Duncan and others presented in a 1984 book written by the staff of the Institute for Social Research, which conducted the PSID; see *Years of Poverty, Years of Plenty* (Ann Arbor, Mich.: Institute for Social Research, 1984). Duncan et al. emphasize the transient (in-and-out) character of AFDC recipiency. Murray, by contrast, stresses the size, characteristics, and pattern of the long-

term welfare population. Murray's paper, "According to Age: Longitudinal Profiles of AFDC Recipients and the Poor by Age Group," was prepared for a working seminar on family and American welfare policy under the auspices of the American Enterprise Institute, Washington, D.C., September 1986.

Chapter 2

1. Harold D. Laswell, "The Policy Orientation," in *The Policy Sciences,* Daniel Lerner and Harold D. Laswell, eds. (Stanford, Calif.: Stanford University Press, 1951), p. 15.

2. Daniel Lerner, "Social Science: Whence and Whither?" in *The Meaning of the Social Sciences,* Daniel Lerner, ed. (Gloucester, Mass.: Peter Smith, 1973), p. 14.

3. Ibid. Carol H. Weiss has written extensively about the enthusiasm of the early advocates of social research as an input to public policymaking. See, for example, her introductory essay in *Using Social Research in Public Policy Making,* Carol H. Weiss, ed. (Lexington, Mass.: Lexington Books, 1977).

4. Robert S. Lynd, *Knowledge for What? The Place of Social Science in American Culture* (Princeton: Princeton University Press, 1948), p. 19.

5. Robert H. Haveman, *Poverty Policy and Poverty Research: The Great Society and the Social Sciences* (Madison: University of Wisconsin Press, 1987), pp. 4–5.

6. Walter W. Heller, *New Dimensions of Political Economy* (Cambridge, Mass.: Harvard University Press, 1966), pp. 1–2.

7. U.S. Bureau of the Budget, Bulletin no. 68–9, 12 April 1968, in *Government Budgeting: Theory, Process, Politics,* Albert C. Hyde and Jay M. Shafritz, eds. (Oak Park, Ill.: Moore, 1978), pp. 129, 130.

8. Allen Schick, "A Death in the Bureaucracy," in Hyde and Shafritz, *Government Budgeting,* p. 191.

9. Carlos Fuentes, *The Hydra Head* (New York: Farrar, Straus & Giroux, 1978), p. 41. I am indebted to Eli Ginzberg for suggesting this quotation.

10. Lester C. Thurow, *Dangerous Currents: The State of Economics* (New York: Random House, 1983), p. 8.

11. Ibid., p. xvi.

12. Wassily Leontief, "Theoretical Assumptions and Nonobserved Facts," *American Economic Review* 61 (March 1971):4, 6.

13. Wassily Leontief, "Letters," *Science* 217 (9 July 1982):217.

14. Ibid.

15. Andrew M. Karmarck, *Economics and the Real World* (Oxford: Basil Blackwell, 1983), pp. 8, 9, 18.

16. Barbara R. Bergmann, "The Failures of Chair-Bound Science," *New York Times,* 12 December 1982, p. F-3.

17. Robert Kuttner, "The Poverty of Economics," *Atlantic Monthly,* February 1985, pp. 74, 76, emphasis added.

18. See Robert E. Lucas, Jr., "Expectations and the Neutrality of Money," *Journal of Economic Theory* (April 1972), pp. 103–24.

19. Albert O. Hirschman, "Against Parsimony: Three Easy Ways of Complicating

Some Categories of Economic Discourse," *Bulletin of the American Academy of Arts and Sciences* 37 (May 1984):11. Similar reactions to economic forecasts occur in the private sector. A 15 July 1987 article in the *New York Times* on the "Economic Scene" quoted the head of an executive search firm as saying, "Our activity level on economists is very low." Many companies, it was noted, have eliminated or reduced the size of their economics departments. "They have done so as cost-cutting measures, but also out of disillusionment with forecasts that in recent years often failed to anticipate the twists of the uncertain American economy." See Louis Uchitelle, "The Shift from Forecasting," *New York Times,* 15 July 1987, p. D-2.

20. Donald N. McCloskey, "The Rhetoric of Economics," *Journal of Economic Literature* 21 (June 1983):484.

21. Ibid., p. 482.

22. Charles L. Schultze, *The Politics and Economics of Public Spending* (Washington, D.C.: The Brookings Institution, 1968).

23. Ibid., p. 94. See also Charles E. Lindblom, "The Science of Muddling Through," *Public Administration Review* 19 (Spring 1959):79–88.

24. Bertram M. Gross, "The New Systems Budgeting," in Hyde and Shafritz, *Government Budgeting,* p. 152.

25. Schultze, *Politics,* pp. 85–86.

26. Roland McKean, *Public Spending* (New York: McGraw-Hill, 1968), p. 141.

27. Richard R. Nelson, *The Moon and the Ghetto: An Essay on Public Policy Analysis* (New York: Norton, 1977), p. 32.

28. Henry J. Aaron, *Politics and the Professors: The Great Society in Perspective* (Washington, D.C.: The Brookings Institution, 1978), pp. 4, 32. The phrase "forensic social science" is attributed by Aaron to Alice M. Rivlin.

29. Ibid., p. 159.

30. Henry J. Aaron, comment, in *Social Experimentation,* Jerry A. Hausman and David A. Wise, eds. (Chicago: University of Chicago Press, 1985), p. 277.

31. See Sar A. Levitan and Gregory Wurzburg, *Evaluating Federal Programs: An Uncertain Act* (Kalamazoo, Mich.: W. E. Upjohn Institute for Employment Research, 1979). Statement provided by the authors.

32. Richard F. Elmore, "Knowledge Development under the Youth Employment Demonstration Projects Act, 1977–1981," National Research Council, National Academy of Science, Washington, D.C., January 1985, paper prepared for the Committee of Youth Employment, p. 87.

33. Charles Murray, *Losing Ground: American Social Policy, 1950–1980* (New York: Basic Books, 1984), pp. 222, 223, 227–28.

34. Ibid., p. 35.

35. Ibid., emphasis added. Murray's omission of economists must have been a momentary mental lapse.

36. Ibid., p. 36.

37. Gary Burtless and Robert H. Haveman, "Policy Lessons from Three Labor Market Experiments," in *Employment and Training R&D: Lessons Learned and Future Directions,* R. Thayne Robson, ed. (Kalamazoo, Mich.: W. E. Upjohn Institute for Employment Research, 1984), p. 128.

38. Ibid., emphasis added. Burtless has softened his position on the value of social experiments. See Burtless and Larry L. Orr, "Are Classical Experiments Needed for Manpower Policy?" *Journal of Human Resources* 21 (Fall 1986):606–39.

Chapter 3

1. Steven V. Roberts, "House and Senate Conferees Settle on $4.6 Billion Employment Plan," *New York Times*, 22 March 1983, emphasis added, pp. 1, 9.

2. Thomas D. Cook and Donald T. Campbell, *Quasi-Experimentation: Design and Analysis Issues for Field Settings* (Chicago: Rand-McNally, 1979), p. 6.

3. Robert A. Levine, "How and Why the Experiments Came About," in *Work Incentives and Income Guarantees: The New Jersey Negative Income Tax Experiment*, Joseph A. Pechman and P. Michael Timpane, eds. (Washington, D.C.: The Brookings Institution, 1975), p. 16.

4. Ibid. p. 21. The delay of this announcement due to Congress's Labor Day recess was especially ironic in this case.

5. Ibid., p. 25.

6. Felicity Skidmore, "Operational Design of the Experiment," in Pechman and Timpane, *Work Incentives*, p. 45.

7. Gilbert Y. Steiner, "Reform Follows Reality: The Growth of Welfare," in *The Great Society: Lessons for the Future*, Eli Ginzberg and Robert M. Solow, eds. (New York: Basic Books, 1974), pp. 47–65.

8. Daniel P. Moynihan, *The Politics of a Guaranteed Income: The Nixon Administration and the Family Assistance Plan* (New York: Random House, 1973), chapter 7, "Congress: The Senate," pp. 509–12.

9. Vincent J. Burke and Vee Burke, *Nixon's Good Deed: Welfare Reform* (New York: Columbia University Press, 1974), p. 41.

10. As quoted in Morton Hunt, *Profiles of Social Research: The Scientific Study of Human Interactions* (New York: Russell Sage Foundation, 1985), p. 292.

11. Gary Burtless and Robert H. Haveman, "Policy Lessons from Three Labor Market Experiments," in *Employment and Training R&D: Lessons Learned and Future Directions*, R. Thayne Robson, ed. (Kalamazoo, Mich.: W. E. Upjohn Institute for Employment Research, 1984), p. 108.

12. Daniel Patrick Moynihan, *Family and Nation* (New York: Harcourt Brace Jovanovich, 1986), p. 151.

13. Specifically, analysis of the SRI data by Glen C. Cain casts doubt on the initial interpretation of the effect of the SIME/DIME experiments on family stability. See Glen C. Cain, "Negative Income Tax Experiments and the Issues of Marital Stability and Family Composition," in *Lessons from the Income Maintenance Experiments*, Alicia H. Munnell, ed., proceedings of a conference held in September 1986 (Boston: Federal Reserve Bank of Boston, 1987).

14. Hearings before the Subcommittee on Public Assistance, Committee on Finance, U.S. Senate, *Welfare Research and Experimentation*, 15–17 November 1978 (Washington, D.C.: U.S. Government Printing Office, 1978), pp. 96–97.

15. Moynihan, *Family and Nation*, p. 152.

16. Hearings, 1978, p. 82.

17. Peter H. Rossi, "A Critical View of the Analysis of the Nonlabor Force Responses," in Pechman and Timpane, *Work Incentives*, p. 161.

18. Lee Rainwater, "Sociological Lessons from the Negative Income Tax Experiments: A Sociological View," in Munnell, *Lessons*, p. 194.

19. See Garland E. Allen, Jerry J. Fitts, and Evelyn S. Glatt, "The Experimental Housing Allowance Program," in *Do Housing Allowances Work?* Katherine Bradbury

and Anthony Downs, eds. (Washington, D.C.: The Brookings Institution, 1981), p. 110.

20. Larry O. Orr, "The Health Insurance Study: Experimentation and Health Financing Policy," *Inquiry* 11 (March 1974): 28.

21. Robert H. Brook, John E. Ware, Jr., William Rogers, Emmett B. Keller, Allyson R. Davies, George A. Goldberg, Kathleen N. Lohr, Patricia Camp, and Joseph P. Newhouse, *The Effect of Coinsurance on the Health of Adults: Results from the Rand Health Insurance Experiment* (Santa Monica, Calif.: Rand Corporation, 1985).

22. *A Study of Alternatives in American Education,* 7 vols. (Santa Monica, Calif.: Rand Corporation, 1976–81).

23. See John R. Berrueta-Clement et al., *Changed Lives: The Effects of the Perry Preschool Program on Youths Through Age 19* (Ypsilanti, Mich.: High Scope Press, 1984).

24. See, for example, N. L. Gage, *Teacher Effectiveness and Teacher Education: The Search for a Scientific Basis* (Palo Alto, Calif.: Pacific Books, 1972).

Chapter 4

1. Robert J. LaLonde, "Evaluating the Econometric Evaluations of Training Programs with Experimental Data," Working Paper no. 183, Industrial Relations Section, Princeton University, October 1984, pp. 183.

2. Ibid., p. 67.

3. Orley Ashenfelter, "The Case for Evaluating Training Programs with Randomized Trails," Working Paper no. 203, Industrial Relations Section, Princeton University, January 1986, pp. 1, 8.

4. James J. Heckman, V. Joseph Hotz, and Marcelo Dabos, "Do We Need Experimental Data to Evaluate the Impact of Manpower Training on Earnings?" *Evaluation Review* 11 (August 1987): 395–427.

5. Lampman as quoted in Eli Ginzberg, Richard Nathan, and Robert Solow, "The Lesson of the Supported Work Demonstration," in *The National Supported Work Demonstration,* Robinson G. Hollister, Jr., Peter Kemper, and Rebecca A. Maynard, eds. (Madison: University of Wisconsin Press, 1984), p. 308.

6. Janet C. Quint and James A. Riccio, *The Challenge of Serving Pregnant and Parenting Teens: Lessons from Project Redirection* (New York: Manpower Demonstration Research Corporation, April 1985), p. 15. New MDRC follow-up data for five years indicate positive longer-term impacts of Project Redirection.

7. U.S. General Accounting Office, "CETA Demonstration Provides Lessons on Implementing Youth Programs," *Report to the Congress by the Comptroller General of the United States,* HRD-81-1, 8 December 1980, p. i.

8. See Marshall J. Breger, "Randomized Social Experiments and the Law," in *Solutions to Ethical and Legal Problems in Social Research,* Robert F. Boruch and Joe S. Cecil, eds. (New York: Academic Press, 1983), pp. 106–7.

9. Alice M. Rivlin and P. Michael Timpane, "Introduction and Summary," in *Ethical and Legal Issues of Social Experimentation,* Alice M. Rivlin and P. Michael Timpane, eds. (Washington, D.C.: The Brookings Institution, 1975), p. 15.

10. Ibid., p. 7.

11. Leonard S. Miller et al., *The Comparative Evaluation of the Multipurpose Senior*

Services Project—1981–1982: Final Report (Berkeley: University of California, Multipurpose Senior Services Project Evaluation, August 1984).

12. I am indebted to my MDRC board colleague Eli Ginzberg for having patiently planted the seeds of doubt that have borne fruit in this analysis, although many readers will no doubt quarrel with the position I have taken here. Lloyd Ullman also helped me in working through these issues. Neither Ginzberg nor Ullman are responsible for the statements made in this section.

13. Office of Research and Evaluation, Employment and Training Administration, U.S. Department of Labor, "Evaluation of the Economic Impact of the Job Corps Program," September 1982, p. 230.

14. Michael E. Borus, "Why Do We Keep Inventing Square Wheels? What We Know and Don't Know about Remedial Employment and Training Programs for High School Drop Outs," New York City, paper prepared for the Manpower Demonstration Research Corporation, p. 9.

15. Board of Directors, Manpower Demonstration Research Corporation, *Summary and Findings of the National Supported Work Demonstration* (Cambridge, Mass.: Ballinger, 1980), p. 135.

16. I am indebted to Lloyd Ullman for suggesting the expert witness metaphor.

Chapter 5

1. Lee S. Friedman, "An Interim Evaluation of the Supported Work Experiment," *Policy Analysis* 3 (Spring 1977): 147–70; and Lee S. Friedman, "The Use of Ex-Addicts to Deliver Local Services: The Supported Work Experiment," in *Urban Problems and Public Policy Choices,* J. Bergman and H. Wiener, eds. (New York: Praeger, 1975), pp. 58–71.

2. Board of Directors, Manpower Demonstration Research Corporation, *Summary and Findings of the National Supported Work Demonstration* (Cambridge, Mass.: Ballinger, 1980), p. 2.

3. Fred C. Doolittle, "Ronald Reagan and Conservative Welfare Reform," Princeton Urban and Regional Research Center, July 1986, p. 3-1.

4. Lou Cannon, *Reagan* (New York: G. P. Putnam's Sons, 1982), p. 183.

5. The food stamp program, begun as a pilot program under Kennedy, was made automatic and universal under Nixon. In effect, it became a mini-negative income tax operating on a uniform basis throughout the country. Also under Nixon, the national welfare programs to aid the aged poor, blind, and disabled were converted into a centralized program with uniform eligibility requirements administered, not by the states as in the past, but by the Social Security Administration. This is the Supplementary Security Income (SSI) program.

6. Data for January 1987. Food stamps reduce these benefit disparities. For example, the combined package (AFDC plus food stamps) is $720 in California and $334 in Mississippi. Figures provided by Velma Burke of the Congressional Research Service of the Library of Congress.

7. Doolittle, "Ronald Reagan," pp. 3–20.

8. A number of studies have been conducted of Reagan's changes in domestic policy. Two studies funded by the Ford Foundation conducted at Princeton University and the Urban Institute have produced reports and articles describing the Reagan changes

and evaluating their effects. See, for example, Richard P. Nathan et al., *Reagan and the States* (Princeton: Princeton University Press, 1987); and George E. Peterson and Carol W. Lewis, eds., *Reagan and the Cities* (Washington, D.C.: Urban Institute Press, 1986).

9. The reference here is to the elimination after four months of a feature of the AFDC program that allowed working recipients to deduct $30 plus of one-third of their earnings each month for purposes of determining their benefit levels. The $30 deduction was later restored. For a study of the effect of these related changes, see *Final Report: Evaluation of the 1981 AFDC Amendments*, submitted to the Office of Family Assistance, Social Security Administration, Department of Health and Human Services, under Task Order 1, Contract no. 600-82-0095, 15 April 1983. See also U.S. General Accounting Office, "An Evaluation of the 1981 AFDC Changes: Initial Analysis," GAO Report PEMD-84-6 (Washington, D.C.: Government Accounting Office, 2 April 1984).

10. Richard M. Nixon, television address on the New Federalism, *Weekly Compilation of Presidential Documents*, week ending Saturday, 9 August 1969, vol. 5, no. 32 (Washington, D.C.: U.S. Government Printing Office), p. 1,111.

11. A job club is a group activity with a trainer-instructor where welfare recipients develop skills in preparing applications, locating job openings, and being interviewed for employment. Often banks of telephones are used in the job search, and in some cases training sessions for job interviews are videotaped as part of an instruction-feedback process. The Manpower Demonstration Research Corporation (MDRC) has issued several reports on this demonstration. See Barbara Goldman, Judith Gueron, Joseph Ball, Marilyn Price with Daniel Friedlander, and Gayle Hamilton, *California: The Demonstration of State Work/Welfare Initiatives, Preliminary Findings from the San Diego Job Search and Work Experience Demonstration* (New York: MDRC, February 1984); Barbara Goldman, Daniel Friedlander, Judith Gueron, David Long with Gayle Hamilton, and Gregory Hoerz, *California: The Demonstration of State Work/Welfare Initiatives, Findings from the San Diego Job Search and Work Experience Demonstration* (New York: MDRC, May 1985); and Barbara Goldman, Daniel Friedlander, and David Long, *California: The Demonstration of State Work/Welfare Initiatives, Final Report* (New York: MDRC, February 1986).

12. Sanctioning procedures vary in these demonstrations. Usually, they involved a partial reduction of the family's welfare benefit for a period of time. Welfare recipients can also be required to have social workers manage their finances as a sanction for noncompliance. For a discussion of this general issue, see Lawrence M. Mead, *Beyond Entitlement: The Social Obligations of Citizenship* (New York: Free Press, 1986).

13. For a discussion of the findings from these demonstrations, see Judith M. Gueron, *Work Initiatives for Welfare Recipients: Lessons from a Multi-State Experiment* (New York: Manpower Demonstration Research Corporation, 1986).

Chapter 6

1. Eugene Bardach, *The Implementation Game: What Happens When a Bill Becomes a Law* (Cambridge, Mass.: MIT Press, 1977), p. 3.

2. Clinton Rossiter, *The American Presidency* (New York: New American Library, 1956), p. 42.

3. Jeffrey L. Pressman and Aaron Wildavsky, eds., *Implementation*, 3d ed. (Berkeley: University of California Press, 1984), p. 254.

4. James G. March and Johan P. Olsen, "The New Institutionalism: Organizational Factors in Political Life," *American Political Science Review* 78 (1984): 734–49.

5. Robert A. Scott and Arnold R. Shore, *Why Sociology Does Not Apply: A Study of the Use of Sociology in Social Policy* (New York: Elsevier, 1979), pp. 12, 28.

6. Nathan Kaplan and Stephen D. Nelson, "On Being Useful: The Nature and Consequences of Psychological Research on Social Problems," in *The Use and Abuse of Social Science, Behavioral Research and Policy Making*, Irving Louis Horowitz, ed. (New Brunswick, N.J.: Transaction Books, 1975), p. 154.

7. Thomas F. Pettigrew, "Can Social Scientists Be Effective Actors in the Policy Arena?" in *Social Science and Social Policy*, R. Lance Shotland and Melvin M. Mark, eds. (Beverly Hills, Calif.: Sage Publications, 1985), p. 132.

Chapter 7

1. Statement made by David B. Swoap, Secretary, Health and Welfare Agency, state of California, Sacramento, Calif., 24 September 1985.

2. Ibid. The San Diego work/welfare study conducted by MDRC included a survey asking participants about their attitude toward a welfare work requirement. Recipients interviewed six months after entering the work-experience component of San Diego's work/welfare demonstration were asked how fair is it that "you must accept a job assignment in order to receive or keep receiving [welfare] benefits?" Of the 49 respondents, 84 percent said, "It's perfectly fair." A larger sample in a related survey produced similar results. Of 311 persons interviewed on the general question of the fairness of a welfare work requirement, 69 percent of those aware of the requirement said it was fair. See Barbara Goldman, Daniel Friedlander, Judith Gueron, David Long with Gayle Hamilton, and Gregory Hoerz, *California: The Demonstration of State Work/Welfare Initiatives, Findings from the San Diego Job Search and Work Experience Demonstration* (New York: Manpower Demonstration Research Corporation, May 1985), chapter 4, "Program Requirements and Noncompliance."

3. John Wallace and David Long, *GAIN: Planning and Early Implementation* (New York: Manpower Demonstration Research Corporation, 1987), p. 29.

4. Ibid., pp. v, vi.

5. Ibid., p. ix, emphasis added.

6. Ibid., pp. xiii, xvi.

7. "GAIN News," Sacramento, Calif., 24 April 1987, p. 1.

8. Richard C. Paddock, "State Finds 57% on Welfare Lack Basic Job Skills," *Los Angeles Times*, 27 April 1987, p. 1.

9. Gordon Berlin and Andrew Sum, "American Standards of Living, Family Welfare and the Basic Skills Crisis," New York City, Ford Foundation, December 1986.

10. Gary Richards, "Three-Fourths of Those in Workfare in Santa Clara County Lack Skills," *San Jose Mercury News*, 26 July 1987, p. 1-A.

11. Wallace and Long, *GAIN: Planning and Early Implementation*, p. 40.

Chapter 8

1. Thomas D. Cook and Donald T. Campbell, *Quasi-Experimentation: Design and Analysis Issues for Field Settings* (Chicago: Rand-McNally, 1979), p. 7.

2. Fuller definitions of the categories of effects used in this study are contained in Richard P. Nathan, Allen D. Manvel, Susannah E. Calkins, et al., *Monitoring Revenue Sharing* (Washington, D.C.: The Brookings Institution, 1975). The analysis of the distributional effects of the program was conducted by Allen Manvel, who had previously served as the chief of the Governments Division of the U.S. Bureau of the Census.

3. For a discussion of other studies, see ibid., chapter 9.

4. For a full description of the methodology and findings of this statistical study, see Charles F. Adams, Jr., and Dan Crippen, "The Fiscal Impact of Revenue Sharing on Local Governments," Office of Revenue Sharing, U.S. Department of the Treasury, May 1978. A similar complementarity study is described in more detail in the next chapter on evaluation research in the field of employment and training.

5. See Nathan, Manvel, Calkins, et al., *Monitoring;* and Richard P. Nathan, Charles F. Adams, Jr., et al., *Revenue Sharing: The Second Round* (Washington, D.C.: The Brookings Institution, 1977).

6. Nathan, Manvel, Calkins, et al., *Monitoring,* p. 184.

7. Subcommittee on Revenue Sharing, Committee on Finance, U.S. Senate, *General Revenue Sharing,* 16 April 1975, p. 50.

8. Testimony, Richard Nathan, Allen Manvel, and Susannah Calkins, Subcommittee on Intergovernmental Relations, Committee on Government Operations, U.S. Senate, *Revenue Sharing,* 5 June 1974, p. 426.

Chapter 9

1. For a summary discussion of this research, see Paul R. Dommel et al., *Decentralizing Urban Policy: Case Studies in Community Development* (Washington, D.C.: The Brookings Institution, 1982).

2. George E. Johnson, "Evaluation Questions for the Comprehensive Employment and Training Act of 1973," Framework for Evaluation Paper no. 2 (Washington, D.C.: U.S. Department of Labor, Office of Assistant Secretary for Policy, Evaluation, and Research, July 1974).

3. The design and findings of the Brookings study were summarized by Richard P. Nathan, Robert F. Cook, V. Lane Rawlins, et al., *Public Service Employment: A Field Evaluation* (Washington, D.C.: The Brookings Institution, 1981). See also Robert F. Cook, Charles F. Adams, Jr., V. Lane Rawlins, *Public Service Employment: The Experience of a Decade* (Kalamazoo, Mich.: W. E. Upjohn Institute for Employment Research, 1985). Four rounds of field research were conducted for this study: in July 1977 at the beginning of the Carter administration's expansion of the program; in December 1977 at the height of this enrollment buildup; in December 1979; and in December 1980.

4. See Nathan, Cook, Rawlins, et al., *Public Service,* chapter 2.

5. Charles F. Adams, Jr., Robert Cook, and Arthur J. Maurice, "A Pooled Time-Series Analysis of the Job-Creation Impact of Public Service Employment Grants to Large Cities," *Journal of Human Resources* 17 (1983): 283–94.

6. Later statistical studies of the intergovernmental effects of the CETA public service employment program corrected for this factor. See Lauri J. Bassi and Alan Fechter, "The Implications for Fiscal Substitution and Occupational Displacement under Expanded CETA Title VI," Technical Analysis Paper no. 65 (Washington, D.C.: U.S. Department of Labor, Office of the Assistant Secretary for Policy, Evaluation, and Research, March 1979).

7. For examples of the implementation studies, see Grace A. Franklin and Randall B. Ripley, *CETA: Politics and Policy, 1973–1982* (Knoxville: University of Tennessee Press, 1984); and William Mirengoff and Lester Rindler, *The Comprehensive Employment and Training Act: Impacts on People, Places, Programs, an Interim Report* (Washington, D.C.: National Academy of Sciences, 1976).

8. "Continuous Longitudinal Manpower Survey: The Impact of CETA on Participant Earnings," Working Paper no. 2, Entrants During the First Half of 1975 (Washington, D.C.: U.S. Department of Labor, Employment and Training Administration, June 1980, prepared by Westat, Inc., Rockville, Md.), p. xviii.

9. "Continuous Longitudinal Manpower Survey," Net Impact Report no. 1, Supplement no. 1, "The Impact of CETA on 1978 Earnings: Participants in Selected Program Activities Who Entered CETA During FY 1976" (Washington, D.C.: U.S. Department of Labor, Employment and Training Administration, July 1982, prepared by Westat, Inc., Rockville, Md.), p. 1-3.

Chapter 10

1. Study Project on Social Research and Development, National Research Council, *The Federal Investment in Knowledge of Social Problems* (Washington, D.C.: National Academy of Sciences, 1978).

2. As quoted in *Science News* 115 (31 March 1979): 213.

INDEX

Index